"Scientists tell one that proof of life is rooted in being able to discern that something has or is changing. As a theologian and Pastor for over 25 years, I declare this fact applies to more than science. "A Changed Mindset" offers the reader, both believer and otherwise, the chance to substantively explore this concept on an organizational, spiritual, and personal level. By tackling the theological premises and intersections of such sacred thoughts as salvation, destiny, relationship, and divine purpose. Dr. Althea Phillips takes us on a unique and much needed journey. Confidently, I recommend reading this book as part of your spiritual walk-through life. It will bless, enrich, and change you for the better."

—Rev Adolphus C. Lacey, PhD
Bethany Baptist Church of Brooklyn, New York

A CHANGED MINDSET

Dr. Althea L. Phillips

CLAY BRIDGES
PRESS

A Changed Mindset

Copyright © 2022 by Dr. Althea L. Phillips

Published by Clay Bridges in Houston, TX
www.ClayBridgesPress.com

All rights reserved. No part of this publication may be reproduced, stored in a retrieval system, or transmitted in any form by any means, electronic, mechanical, photocopy, recording, or otherwise, without the prior permission of the publisher, except as provided for by USA copyright law.

eISBN: 978-1-68488-016-4
ISBN: 978-1-68488-017-1

Special Sales: Most Clay Bridges titles are available in special quantity discounts. Custom imprinting or excerpting can also be done to fit special needs. For standard bulk orders, go to www.claybridgesbulk.com. For specialty press or large orders, contact Clay Bridges at info@claybridgespress.com.

To my mother, Rev. Jeannette Phillips, who taught me how to defend my core values and encouraged me to write.

To my beloved baby sister, Elizabeth, my friend and inspiration who encouraged me to continue writing despite my learning disability; and to my older sister, Deborah, who is a living example of trusting God in difficult times.

To my daughters—Jennifer, Stephanie, Christine, and Althea.

To my granddaughters—Zariana, Susan, Zoey, and Aleah.

To my sister-in-law Dr. Glenetta Phillips who is often looked upon as the rock in adversities.

To my daughter in-law Melissa who has demonstrated time after time what a friend we have in Jesus.

TABLE OF CONTENTS

Introduction	1
Chapter 1: But Who Do You Say That I Am?	3
Chapter 2: Let This Go to Your Head	21
Chapter 3: "I Can Do All Things"	35
Chapter 4: It Begins at Ground Zero	45
Chapter 5: Set Up for a Comeback	53
Chapter 6: Faith Is a Different Pair of Lenses	59
Chapter 7: Mary, Why Are You Weeping?	77
Chapter 8: God Is Predetermined	85
Chapter 9: God Is Mindful	99
Chapter 10: The Mindset That Feeds	105
Chapter 11: Jesus, the Church, and Religion's Activities	117
Chapter 12: Delivery	123
Chapter 13: Beautiful Feet	133
Chapter 14: A Changed Mindset View of the Kingdom of God	141
Final Notes	151
Special Thanks	153

INTRODUCTION

And be not conformed to this world: but be ye transformed by the renewing of your mind, that ye may prove what is that good, and acceptable, and perfect, will of God.

—Rom. 12:2 KJV

The result of thinking like Jesus is a unique mindset found in the bride of Christ. Having the mindset of the bride of Christ Jesus means sharing an intimate and personal relationship with Jesus by seeking first the kingdom of heaven and its righteousness. My motivation for writing this book is the hope that followers of Jesus Christ will become more aware of the importance of a changed mindset following the transformation process. A 21st century virgin mindset is a thought process that has not yet come to know the importance of seeking with diligence a personal, intimate relationship with Jesus. The process of a changed mindset empowers the bride of Christ—men and women seeking to have a more intimate conversation with God.

Seeking the kingdom of heaven and its righteousness will also help others know their true purpose as His bride. Jesus came to transform the mindsets of 21st century virgins in order to establish a personal, intimate relationship with them as their bridegroom. The mindset of the 21st century virgin often gets stuck at the altar of salvation. They often first seek religious traditions and not a personal, intimate relationship with Jesus. That can make it very challenging for them to transform and change into a new creature in Christ Jesus.

Chapter 1

BUT WHO DO YOU SAY THAT I AM?

I n Haggai 1:2–9, God used the prophet Haggai to hold the church accountable for becoming disorganized and spiritually undernourished as the body of Christ. "Ye looked for much, and, lo, it came to little; and when ye brought it home, I did blow upon it. Why? saith the LORD of hosts. Because of mine house that is waste, and ye run every man unto his own house" (Hag. 1:9 KJV). The 21st century virgin's thought process cannot understand its purpose until they can comprehend God's plan for their life as their only essential way of living. Moreover, until God's plan is revealed, their purpose remains a mystery from Him who gives life its true meaning.

Jesus often used parables to help illustrate or demonstrate kingdom concepts. One concept is the understanding of the kingdom of heaven and the vital role it plays in knowing your purpose.

> *Or what woman, having ten silver coins, if she loses one coin, does not light a lamp, sweep the house, and search carefully until she finds it? And when she has found it, she calls her friends and neighbors together, saying, "Rejoice with me, for*

A CHANGED MINDSET

I have found the piece which I lost!" Likewise, I say to you, there is joy in the presence of the angels of God over one sinner who repents.
—Luke 15:8–10

Jesus used this parable to illustrate how heaven celebrates when one lost coin is found. To the mindset of the 21st century virgin, when finding purpose, it increases its value to the follower because what was lost is now found.

The other day, I shared with my oldest son, Tyrone, that the mindset of Jesus is needed in order to enter into a spiritual dimension of the kingdom of God. However, there is a process in knowing your purpose in the kingdom of God. The kingdom of God is a mindset that thinks like Jesus. I told Tyrone a story. I said to imagine yourself at home in your kitchen, and a thought or calling crosses your mind that you need your car keys to move your car. You know your keys are upstairs on your nightstand. You go upstairs and enter your bedroom, but suddenly you forget what you are looking for. You search your mind, and without any recall, you fail to remember why you went upstairs. Second Corinthians 5:7–9 says, "For we walk by faith, not by sight. We are confident, yes, well pleased rather to be absent from the body and to be present with the Lord. Therefore we make it our aim, whether present or absent, to be well pleasing to Him."

I further explain to Tyrone that as you continue to look around your room, hoping you will find clues to help you recall why you came upstairs, you become frustrated and begin to doubt yourself and that you have a purpose for entering your bedroom. Yet something inside of you won't let you give up.

Needless to say, the process in knowing that you were called to do something is a faith journey. It is faith that speaks to your thought process that you were called to do something. It is not the frustrations of going through the process of why you are called that God sees but how you use faith in the frustrations. It's the walking by faith when followers are challenged and not always overcoming the challenges of frustrations that please God. Jeremiah 29:11 says, "For I know the thoughts that I think toward you, says the LORD, thoughts of peace and not of evil, to give you a future and a hope."

God doesn't become discouraged when we are faced with adversity. In the process, He checks our spiritual pulse to see how effectively our faith is working. To find our purpose is a search that is not done through our natural eyes or the carnality of our thoughts, but rather by faith. It is faith that opens our mindset to please God regardless of what dimension we are currently in.

Often followers, when seeking their purpose by faith, find themselves leaving one dimension and entering into another dimension. That change brings uncertainty, but God is faithful. Seeking the kingdom of God and its righteousness becomes the pathway of leading people from one dimension into another as they are transformed into having a mindset like Christ Jesus. A mindset like Jesus empowers individuals to believe and have faith in God's Word while answering the call He has for their purpose. Psalm 37:23 says, "The steps of a *good* man are ordered by the LORD, and He delights in his way."

The journey or process in seeking why you where sent to find your purpose is guided by the Holy Spirit, and the steps God ordered are created by faith. The steps and the Holy Spirit facilitate your thought process into a total recall of your purpose and calling. Consequently, you must first believe in your mind that there is a reason you answered the call to move from one dimension to another.

As a result of Tyrone's search, he did recall what he was sent to do. He found his car keys and moved his car. Nevertheless, the knowledge of his purpose appeared to be lost in his thought process. Jesus as the Good Shepherd by faith guided Tyrone's path into finding what appeared to be lost in his way of thinking. In the story, I explained what kept Tyrone in his room while seeking a lost thought he knew in his heart he was sent to do something. What he believed became the driving force of his faith, which empowered him to seek the purpose for why he was called to his bedroom. John 10:27–28 says, "My sheep hear My voice, and I know them, and they follow Me. And I give unto them eternal life, and they shall never perish; neither shall anyone snatch them out of My hand."

The kingdom of heaven is where God's Word is at work. Jesus the Living Word of God is omnipresent, and the foundation of the kingdom of God and heaven is His Word. Having that same mind of Jesus Christ empowers us to have a mindset like the bride of Christ who perceives the kingdom of heaven as a way of thinking in another dimension. Luke 10:11 says, "Nevertheless know this, that the kingdom of God has come near you." Moving from one dimension to another in your thought process of seeking your calling and purpose takes place in the natural while you are having a spiritual experience.

Your old way of thinking is changed as you enter into a spiritual dimension while still living in the natural. "I beseech you therefore, brethren, by the mercies of God, that you present your bodies a living sacrifice, holy, acceptable to God, *which is* your reasonable service. And do not be conformed to this world, but be transformed by the renewing of your mind, that you may prove what *is* that good and acceptable and perfect will of God" (Rom. 12:1–2). It is through a changed mindset that people are empowered by the Holy Spirit to be transformed and to have purpose.

> *And we know that all things work together for good to those who love God, to those who are the called according to* His *purpose. For whom He foreknew, He also predestined to be conformed to the image of His Son, that He might be the firstborn among many brethren. Moreover whom He predestined, these He also called; whom He called, these He also justified; and whom He justified, these He also glorified.*
> —Rom. 8:28–30

Everything in life is originated by God who is omniscient, including wisdom and understanding. Understanding is revealed to others by revelation. God's strategic plan makes all things good and in accordance with His intent for them who love Him and who are called for a purpose.

BUT WHO DO YOU SAY THAT I AM?

The clothes you are wearing came from a thought from a designer. Most designers or creators are very passionate about their work, vision, and purpose. This passion is transferred into their work of art or creations. When a designer is working from a thought or a vision, it's not until it's revealed or illustrated on paper that others have a clear understanding of it before it's called to go into production. Revelation empowers others to understand God's purpose or calling for their life.

There is a personal relationship between the designer and the purpose of their design. A designer or a creator must personally interact effectively with the tools used to illustrate their thoughts or vision in hopes that their idea serves a purpose for others. Sometimes as part of God's plan to perfect you, He will move people, places, and circumstances on your behalf and for His glory. To be transformed from a 21st century virgin mindset to the mindset of the bride of Christ is a design's original plan that is guaranteed to work. Nevertheless, we have to believe that faith works. The footsteps of a good person are ordered and designed to bring them into their purpose. In the story of Tyrone and his total recall of remembering why he was called upstairs, he hoped for something he could relate to or have a relationship with that would jar his memory and lead him to his calling or purpose. Hebrews 11:1 says, "Now faith is the substance of things hoped for, the evidence of things not seen." There was nothing in Tyrone's room to help jar his memory, but he held on to his faith until he remembered what he was called to do.

Many followers understood Jesus as a profound religious leader. Since He was revealed as the Son of God by faith and by the power of the Holy Spirit, His purpose becomes more understood by some as their personal Lord and Savior. The 21st century virgin's mindset is easily distracted by religious activities. This way of thinking makes it difficult for a mindset to seek an intimate relationship with Jesus.

> *When Jesus came into the region of Caesarea Philippi, He asked His disciples, saying, "Who do men say that I, the Son of Man, am?" So they said, "Some say John the Baptist, some Elijah, and others Jeremiah or one of the prophets."*

A CHANGED MINDSET

> *He said to them, "But who do you say that I am?" Simon Peter answered and said, "You are the Christ, the Son of the living God." Jesus answered and said to him, "Blessed are you, Simon Bar-Jonah, for flesh and blood has not revealed this to you, but My Father who is in heaven."*
> —Matt. 16:13–17

In Hosea 4:6, we read that God's people are destroyed from a lack of knowledge: "My people are destroyed for lack of knowledge. Because you have rejected knowledge, I also will reject you from being priest for Me; Because you have forgotten the law of your God, I also will forget your children." God is omniscient in His planning and to every creation He gave purpose.

Proverbs 29:18 tells us that where there is no vision, the people perish. The church was a hot mess in the book of Haggai because of poor planning and lack of vision, similar to many churches today that represent the mindset of a 21st century virgin. Without vision, the people die. Without vision, there is no mobility. As a follower, you owe it to yourself to seek God's plan for your life and your purpose, having the same mind that's in Christ Jesus.

God's plan and purpose for your life have been established since the beginning. Your job is to open the door and allow God to enter and reveal His plan to you by the way of process. This thought process fosters followers to be ready for the Master's use in a dimension that can only be entered with a changed mindset. God is telling us in Haggai that the reason we do not already have life abundantly as He promised is because we have lost sight of His plan. Our true identify within ourselves becomes illuminated as followers seek first the kingdom of God and its righteousness.

As part of His creation, God planned for the church to be a body of believers working together as living examples of his Word.

> *For I know the thoughts that I think toward you, says the* Lord, *thoughts of peace and not of evil, to give you a future and a hope. Then you will call upon Me and go and pray to*

> *Me, and I will listen to you. And you will seek Me and find Me, when you search for Me with all your heart. I will be found by you, says the Lord, and I will bring you back from your captivity; I will gather you from all the nations and from all the places where I have driven you, says the Lord, and I will bring you to the place from which I cause you to be carried away captive.*
>
> —Jer. 29:11–14

First things first—get the house of God inside you free from waste and cleaned and organized for the Master's use.

But how can we continue to go on with our daily lives knowing that God's house within us is in such disarray? God's plan for our lives is to maintain the church as the body of Christ. We are to care for His body, which repents from the heart. We should not limit ourselves by our tithes and offerings; we should love and support one another, from picking debris up off the floor when it isn't yours or holding the door open for others to pass through first. These are just a few things we can do as individuals without being asked. However, most important is living out God's greatest commandment—to love Him with all our hearts, souls, and minds, and to love one another as we love ourselves.

God is a designer who has created homes, communities, families, technology, and, most of all, a plan and a purpose for your life. You are only anointed to build what God has already planned for you to build. Nevertheless, it is not by your strength or might but by God's grace that you are empowered to create. Honor Him by letting Christ become the Lord of your life. What is the motivation that takes us from a wasted house to a house where God is glorified and the name of Jesus Christ is lifted up? Where there is hope, there is love.

> *Love never fails. But whether* there are *prophecies, they will fail; whether* there are *tongues, they will cease; whether* there is *knowledge, it will vanish away. For we know in part and we prophesy in part. But when that which is perfect has*

A CHANGED MINDSET

come, then that which is in part will be done away. When I was a child, I spoke as a child, I understood as a child, I thought as a child; but when I became a man, I put away childish things. For now we see in a mirror, dimly, but then face to face. Now I know in part, but then I shall know just as I also am known. And now abide faith, hope, love, these three; but the greatest of these is love.

—1 Cor. 13:8–13

The physical church is a type of conduit used as an outside support system. God's love facilitates the bride of Christ in fulfilling their purpose. Inasmuch, the transformation process leaves behind the old mindset of the 21st century virgin to a new way of thinking. We as the body of believers must demonstrate brotherly love and become the solid foundation on which that love is promoted. Love is the foundation that supports the church. Followers are called to love one another the way Christ loves His bride. The 21st century virgin's thought process moves away from empty religious activities to an intimate relationship with Christ. In 1 John 4:20, God asks us how we can say that we love Him whom we have not seen and refuse to love people we see all the time. The real breakthrough after salvation is the internal struggle from changing from the old mindset to the new mindset of the bride of Christ. Being saved is the easy part since Jesus already paid the price and stands at the door, waiting for us to have a personal relationship with Him as His chosen vessels. Romans 4:17 says, "(As it is written, I have made thee a father of many nations,) before him whom he believed, even God, who quickeneth the dead, and calleth those things which be not as though they were."

It's with the bride of Christ mindset that people get up and move from the altar of salvation and begin the journey of seeking the kingdom of God first as a step in having a personal relationship with Jesus. This is the first step of transforming our mindset into the bride of Christ. Seeking His kingdom is a process of restoration in our relationship with Jesus.

For he chose us in him before the creation of the world to be holy and blameless in his sight. In love he predestined us for adoption to sonship through Jesus Christ, in accordance with his pleasure and will—to the praise of his glorious grace, which he has freely given us in the One he loves. In him we have redemption through his blood, the forgiveness of sins, in accordance with the riches of God's grace that he lavished on us. With all wisdom and understanding, he made known to us the mystery of his will according to his good pleasure, which he purposed in Christ, to be put into effect when the times reach their fulfillment—to bring unity to all things in heaven and on earth under Christ.

—Eph. 1:4–10 NIV

For the earnest expectation of the creation eagerly waits for the revealing of the sons of God. For the creation was subjected to futility, not willingly, but because of Him who subjected it in hope; because the creation itself also will be delivered from the bondage of corruption into the glorious liberty of the children of God. For we know that the whole creation groans and labors with birth pangs together until now. Not only that, but we also who have the firstfruits of the Spirit, even we ourselves groan within ourselves, eagerly waiting for the adoption, the redemption of our body. For we were saved in this hope, but hope that is seen is not hope; for why does one still hope for what he sees? But if we hope for what we do not see, we eagerly wait for it with perseverance. Likewise the Spirit also helps in our weaknesses. For we do not know what we should pray for as we ought, but the Spirit Himself makes intercession for us with groanings which cannot be uttered.

—Rom. 8:19–26

A CHANGED MINDSET

Your anointing, your calling, your destiny have been created to move you toward a more personal relationship with God. Subsequently, it is not the everyday sins we commit that rob us of God after salvation through Christ Jesus. Rather, the greatest sin is to not pursue our destiny to our purpose. Knowing who you are is done through seeking the kingdom of heaven and its righteousness first. When the end of our journey in this life is completed, the greatest disappointment for many followers is not living up to everything that God created them to become. There is an unbalanced spiritual perception that sees religion as more important than relationship and sin more important than destiny or purpose. The church of today often spends too much time and too many resources on admonishing sins that are committed and not enough time and resources on developing, redirecting, and fostering followers to seek the kingdom and discover their purpose and destiny. Matthew 16:15 says, "But who do you say that I am?"

Salvation is essential; however, destiny-seeking is just as important and perhaps more intense because it is a lifelong process as opposed to a moment in true confession that Jesus is Lord. Time is getting shorter as it relates to Jesus's return. We must be about the Father's business more than ever before since the harvest is plentiful but the laborers are few. "For it is with your heart that you believe and are justified, and it is with your mouth that you profess your faith and are saved" (Rom. 10:10 NIV).

For some, it takes close to a lifetime to understand and live out their destiny. The real breakthrough or revelation is when followers see their destinies equally important as God sending His Son to fulfill His destiny. There is a huge profit for followers who learn how to know their destiny. This behavior decreases the risk of hating on others because your focus time is on purpose and how valuable you are in God's plan. Matthew 6:33 (NIV) tells us, "But seek first his kingdom and his righteousness, and all these things will be given to you as well."

Before you were born, God created and planted in seed form your destiny. Your journey in seeking the kingdom of God is the process of knowing the thoughts of God in your own mind. There is an assignment, a calling, a gift that God freely gives to everyone. "For God so loved the world that he gave his one and only Son, that whoever believes in him shall not perish but have eternal life" (John 3:16 NIV).

Jeremiah 1:4–5 (NIV) says, "Before I formed you in the womb I knew you, before you were born I set you apart; I appointed you as a prophet to the nations." In Jeremiah 29:11 (NIV), the prophet tells us, "'For I know the plans I have for you,' declares the Lord, 'plans to prosper you and not to harm you, plans to give you hope and a future.'" These gifts that God has placed in His followers' lives inspire followers to pursue the kingdom of heaven. God has shared in His Word that many are called, but few are chosen. The difference between being called and chosen lies in knowing one's gifts from God and having a true relationship with Him. When the chosen see their gifts, they see a reflection of God's grace and not their personal perception of what they can do for a living. These gifts allow us to reflect on who God is in our lives from day to day. This revelation is like a magnet that draws the bride of Christ closer to God by having a mindset that seeks Him with their hearts, souls, and minds. The bride of Christ mindset knows that by the grace of God, the gifts are activated when they are plugged into their purpose.

The mindset of the 21st century virgin can easily become intoxicated by the benefits of having gifts they don't seek from the Giver of the gifts. The gifts themselves become gods. This mindset fails to see the grace of God and becomes enamored by the gifts instead of the Giver. The mindset of the bride of Christ realizes that the outcome of the process empowers the personal relationship they share through Him by faith. The end result of all situations for the mindset of the bride of Christ is knowing the victory that stems from having a personal relationship with Jesus. Out of the belly flows living water, which is a direct correlation to being plugged into Jesus. Needless to say, because of the relationship, He does not need to ask them, "Where are you?" the way He asked Adam.

The bride of Christ Jesus mindset sees Him as omniscient and a consultant for life's situations. In Luke 9:23 (NIV), we read, "Then he said to them all: 'Whoever wants to be my disciple must deny themselves and take up their cross daily and follow me.'" God sees people with the 21st century virgin mindset as His beloved bride who lacks the mindset of Jesus and who has not developed an intimate relationship with Him through Jesus Christ. One of the best things about the process of seeking God is the revelation of understanding the gift or calling. Understanding the gifts within us mirrors who God is in each gift He has chosen to give them. He called with an all-inclusive and no-regrets promissory note attached. "For the gifts and the calling of God *are* irrevocable" (Rom. 11:29).

Usually when I plan a trip out of the country, I select a vacation resort that is all-inclusive. These spots have much to be desired since management thinks of everything, and all you need to do is show up. Management makes all the necessary calls to assure your stay is everything they promised in their advertisement. The steps God has ordered for us are similar to an all-inclusive resort. They are empowered by His love, and the process of knowing who you are is managed by faith. The kingdom of God encloses the steps in knowing who He is. It is by these steps of faith that individuals know their purpose. In God's Word, He instructs people to seek first the kingdom of God. The process in seeking the kingdom of God first provides people an opportunity to know who God is by the way of process. It is in this hope of knowing the purpose that we were created. "This *is* the day the Lord has made; we will rejoice and be glad in it" (Ps. 118:24).

Understanding the power behind these words empowers the mindset of the bride of Christ Jesus to know that no matter how the day starts, where it begins, or how far it goes, we are more than winners in Him.

> *As it is written, for thy sake we are killed all the day long; we are accounted as sheep for the slaughter. Nay, in all these things we are more than conquerors through him that loved us. For I am persuaded, that neither death, nor life, nor angels, nor principalities, nor powers, nor things present, nor things to come, nor height, nor depth, nor any other creature, shall be able to separate us from the love of God, which is in Christ Jesus our Lord.*
>
> —Rom. 8:36–38 KJV

BUT WHO DO YOU SAY THAT I AM?

A changed mindset that reflects the same mind that is in Christ Jesus sees every day that the Lord has given us opportunities to believe that God is omnipresent and in control of every outcome. Often the challenge for the 21st century virgin mindset is believing in who God said He is when we're faced with challenges in the day that the Lord has made. The Lord's Prayer teaches learners that every day God will provide the bread we need to live by the way of process. Start first by acknowledging God for who He is according to His Word.

> *After this manner therefore pray ye: Our Father which art in heaven, hallowed be thy name. Thy kingdom come, Thy will be done in earth, as it is in heaven. Give us this day our daily bread. And forgive us our debts, as we forgive our debtors. And lead us not into temptation, but deliver us from evil: For thine is the kingdom, and the power, and the glory, for ever. Amen.*
>
> —Matt. 6:9–13 KJV

In this prayer, Jesus gives rise to the message that this is the day that He has made.

The kingdom of God holds valuable information pertaining to who God is. However, seeking Him must be done diligently. People must have every intention of finding Him as their only mission, even at first they cannot trace Him. I once asked my son Tyrone that if he needed to find me, where would he first look. He said jokingly at my job, and then he said at home. I went on to say, "You would look for me at my place of work rather than at home where I live?" It didn't come to me until much later that my home is where I spend most of my hours, and it also happens to be where I work. I live to work, although it is not limited to a job. On the contrary, any type of work I am doing that leads to purpose I consider work. Working toward purpose is a process that needs to be part of our lives all the time while we are awake or asleep. "Thus also faith by itself, if it does not have works, is dead. But someone will say, 'You have faith, and I have works.' Show me your faith without your works, and I will show you my faith by my works. You believe that there is one God. You do well. Even the demons believe—and tremble!" (James 2:17–19).

The Word of God covers our steps, and His promises ensure our destiny. We read in Philippians 4:13 (NIV), "I can do all this through him who gives me strength." And in Hebrews 11:6, we read, "But without faith it is impossible to please him: for he that cometh to God must believe that he is, and that he is a rewarder of them that diligently seek him." Each step God has made for us holds His promises and provisions, which give his followers a reason to rejoice and be glad. The steps uncover God in every aspect of our lives. In short, everything you need to know who you are is in the discovery of who God is at His place of work. Again, in retrospect, my son Tyrone was correct. The best place to find me in having a mindset of a bride of Christ is at work.

In the Lord's Prayer, Jesus teaches us first to acknowledge who God is and then that the kingdom of heaven is our destiny in finding Him at work. God's plan for our lives has already been established in heaven, and we can access that plan here on earth. The daily bread He gives us is his Word, which supersizes our ability to reach our destiny. We must take on the role of Christ in each step we take, demonstrating our love for others through the way we treat them, despite our own selfish feelings. God gave us his Son despite the way the world treated Him. He demonstrated unconditional love. Because we are made in His image and likeness, we are expected to love the unlovable and do whatever it takes to let go of self-righteousness and acknowledge Jesus's righteousness as the only way.

We are made right because of Jesus; however, we need to acknowledge that His rigor must take precedence in our daily lives. Matthew 16:24–26 (NIV) tells us, "Then Jesus said to his disciples, 'Whoever wants to be my disciple must deny themselves and take up their cross and follow me. For whoever wants to save their life will lose it, but whoever loses their life for me will find it. What good will it be for someone to gain the whole world, yet forfeit their soul? Or what can anyone give in exchange for their soul?'"

Our purpose as followers of God is a constant development of a personal relationship with Jesus. During the process of taking on His mindset, we will encounter many challenges. Often in Western culture, religion teaches its followers to fight against challenges through the carnality of their mind. But in truth, our strength and victory lie in overcoming these challenges through our relationship with Jesus. Isaiah 54:17 says, "'No weapon formed against you shall prosper, and every tongue *which* rises against you in judgment you shall condemn. This *is* the heritage of the servants of the Lord, and their righteousness *is* from Me,' says the Lord." This promise is revealed and becomes a force field for the bride of Christ because of her intimate relationship with God through Jesus. Since the very beginning, God was and is always about establishing an intimate relationship with the world, instead of religious activities. Perhaps that is why Jesus asked Peter in Matthew 16:15, "But who do you say that I am?" As followers going through the process of the transformation from the mindset of the 21st century virgin to that of the bride of Christ thought process, we will come to know that revelation is not obtained through the knowledge of flesh and blood. Rather it is given through our intimate relationship with God through Jesus by His Spirit. It is about personally knowing for yourself who God is in you. Again, "Who do you say that I am?"

The transformation process fosters followers to think more effectively in pursuit of their purpose with God. This process increases their capability to live an abundant life as men and women in the body of Christ. Moving forward, transformation facilitates change from a virgin mindset to a bride of Christ mindset or thought process.

> *Then shall the kingdom of heaven be likened unto ten virgins, which took their lamps, and went forth to meet the bridegroom. And five of them were wise, and five were foolish. They that were foolish took their lamps, and took no oil with them: But the wise took oil in their vessels with their lamps. While the bridegroom tarried, they all slumbered and slept. And at midnight there was a cry made, Behold, the bridegroom cometh; go ye out to meet him. Then all those virgins arose, and trimmed their lamps. And the foolish*

A CHANGED MINDSET

> *said unto the wise, Give us of your oil; for our lamps are gone out. But the wise answered, saying, Not so; lest there be not enough for us and you: but go ye rather to them that sell, and buy for yourselves. And while they went to buy, the bridegroom came; and they that were ready went in with him to the marriage: and the door was shut. Afterward came also the other virgins, saying, Lord, Lord, open to us. But he answered and said, Verily I say unto you, I know you not. Watch therefore, for ye know neither the day nor the hour wherein the Son of man cometh.*
> —Matt. 25:1–13 KJV

Similar to the parable of the 10 virgins, the journey in seeking the kingdom of God, although challenging at times, prepares followers to reach their destiny. Five out of the 10 virgins understood that the oil served a purpose in reaching their destiny. The other five were clueless in understanding the connection between the purpose of the oil and their destiny. Salvation and what we were saved to do is also connected as we walk by faith in seeking first the kingdom of God. Engaging yourself fully while seeking the kingdom of God is by no other means than establishing a personal, intimate relationship with God by faith. The Holy Spirit, who is a type of oil in the lamp, ignites the light in guiding people to their purpose and destiny.

The things you learn while going through the journey are spiritual homework assignments that are essential in moving to the next step. These assignments are the steps necessary to move toward destiny. It's not the journey that people reflect on when reaching their purpose; it's the challenging steps in the process of getting there and where lessons are learned. The Holy Spirit throughout this process plays a vital role in revealing lessons that are learned along the way to purpose and destiny.

To become an effective member of the body of Christ, followers need to seek their purpose with a mindset of the bride of Christ. Why is salvation preached and taught more often than how to know and live the purpose God placed in followers? Salvation is essential prior to purpose;

however, it is a short-term goal, and purpose is a long-term goal that calls for commitment and diligence. Romans 10:9 (KJV) says, "That if thou shalt confess with thy mouth the Lord Jesus, and shalt believe in thine heart that God hath raised him from the dead, thou shalt be saved."

Purpose is an essential key ingredient in living an abundant life paired with salvation. Once the door to salvation has been opened, it is the follower's personal responsibility to seek God and by faith allow Him to reveal Himself throughout the process of knowing who you are at your core. We are saved not just from sin but for a purpose. We are set aside to do something no one else is appointed to do. The point of teaching believers the importance of knowing their purpose is to facilitate independence from religious activities.

In addition, it encourages empowerment to work through trials, tribulations, and adversities as part of the process. It also fosters believers to develop an intimate relationship with God through Jesus. In the parable, five virgins were wise, and five were foolish. The five wise virgins understood the importance of pursuing a personal relationship with Christ as individuals. The mindset of the 21st century virgin is at risk of being foolish and not wise. It is not until transformation and change take place that the mindset of the 21st century virgin can see themselves as the head and not the tail. Deuteronomy 28:13 says, "And the Lord will make you the head and not the tail; you shall be above only, and not be beneath, if you heed the commandments of the Lord your God, which I command you today, and are careful to observe them."

Chapter 2

LET THIS GO TO YOUR HEAD

In a 2015 movie *The Blind Side*, Mrs. Tuohy (played by Sandra Bullock) said to Sean "SJ" Tuohy, Jr. (played by Jae Head) after he performed well in a middle school Thanksgiving pageant, "SJ, don't let this go to your head." I often heard this same thing when I was growing up after someone in my family stood out in a performance or did something spectacular at home or at school. The concept behind not letting something go to your head is to prevent individuals from getting too proud in how they see themselves perceived by others.Faith for believers becomes a new way of thinking versus the old way of how things were perceived previously. This new mindset becomes the new way of thinking for people who seek to be the bride of Christ and function effectively in their purpose. The new mindset stops religion from getting in the way of having a personal relationship with God through Jesus simply by letting this go to your head.

God instructs and challenges people to let the same mindset in Jesus be in them. I see this as an opportunity for people who have God's support and blessing to let this mindset go to their head. It can be a game-changer in how they can think more effectively. People often feel they are waiting on God, but rather it is He who is waiting on them to get to know Him who lives, moves, and has a purpose inside of them for their life. Philippians 2:5–7 says, "Let this mind be in you which was also in Christ Jesus, who, being in the form of God, did not consider it robbery to be equal with God, but made Himself of no reputation, taking the form of a bondservant, *and* coming in the likeness of men."

Faith guides individuals to learn to have a conversation *with* God rather than a conversation *to* God. It is this thought process in Jesus that empowers people to pray *with* God. Praying with God stems from having a personal relationship with God and not with religion, which teaches people to pray to God. It is essential for them who seek the kingdom of God and its righteousness, which holds who God is, to know the purpose of why they exist, which lies in transforming your mindset into the same mindset of Jesus. It is this mindset that is the thought process in the bride of Christ, people becoming empowered for every move to be directed by faith.

> *Then Caleb quieted the people before Moses, and said, "Let us go up at once and take possession, for we are well able to overcome it." But the men who had gone up with him said, "We are not able to go up against the people, for they are stronger than we." And they gave the children of Israel a bad report of the land which they had spied out, saying, "The land through which we have gone as spies is a land that devours its inhabitants, and all the people whom we saw in it are men of great stature. There we saw the giants (the descendants of Anak came from the giants); and we were like grasshoppers in our own sight, and so we were in their sight."*
> —Num. 13:30–33

The mindset or thought process governs the behavior of individuals, including their choices. Our thoughts can control our behavior and determine the choices we make. It can be extremely difficult for some people to cope with adversity effectively due to their ineffective thought process. Isaiah 26:3 says, "You will keep *him* in perfect peace, *whose* mind is stayed *on* You, because he trusts in You." To some people, this verse may lead them to believe that God will give them perfect peace because He trusts them. On the contrary, this verse is not about God trusting us but God Himself confirming that we can trust the mindset of Christ Jesus that is in us. As a result, a follower will have a peace that the world cannot take away, including adversities such as COVID-19 or for some people the ineffective reactions toward COVID-19 preventions, precautions, and interventions. John 14:27 says, "Peace I leave with you, My peace I give to you; not as the world gives do I give to you. Let not your heart be troubled, neither let it be afraid." I googled the meaning of the word *trust*, and the Merriam-Webster site read, "to rely on the truthfulness or accuracy of, to place confidence in; to hope or expect confidently." God gives us the ability trust Him, to know we can count on Him because He is faithful and dependable, and we can bank on His word that He will never forsake them who believe in who He is as a provider.

The real truth of the matter is that the biggest adverse effects of COVID-19 are not the loss of loved ones, homes, houses, careers, secured income, or loneliness from isolating yourself from associates, family, and friends. Needless to say, there has been an increase in depression, domestic violence, feeling lonely, and suicidal ideation, just to name a few. But there has been the loss of a vital, vibrant mindset or thought process in treating our neighbor as our brother. The aftermath of COVID-19 as it relates to losses is more than the things people can smell, see, and feel with the human senses. The real virus is the ineffective coping behaviors in others along with the inability to adjust positively to what has turned out to be a new normal.

One way to perceive how faith works is to come to an understanding of the differences between choosing a gift and having a gift choose you. John 15:16 (KJV) says, "Ye have not chosen me, but I have chosen you, and ordained you, that ye should go and bring forth fruit, and that your fruit should remain: that whatsoever ye shall ask of the Father in my name, he may give it you." Growing up as a child, I recall my parents asking me every year what I would like as a gift for my birthday or

A CHANGED MINDSET

for Christmas. My parents were and to this day are very generous in providing their children with at least one or two gifts that we asked for. As I reflect back and try to remember everything I asked for and received from my parents, I realize that those gifts are no longer in my possession. Strangely enough, the gifts that choose us never leave us or get broken, misused, lost, outdated, or stop serving a purpose. Most gifts people give become lost, outdated, broken, or rusty. Maybe they are stolen or lose their value. However, a gift that chooses a person never loses its value or its purpose but only appreciates in its purpose through development or by the means of process. In this process of being chosen, you discover why the gift chose you. Faith is not required when you choose to accept a gift; however, when gifts or callings such as propose choose you, faith is required. When the gift chooses an individual, it rarely comes already developed. Most of the time, it comes in seed form. The seed is not limited to size when compared to the size of the finished project, which in this case are the gifts or the callings. The seed is a process where gifts and callings are developed according to the purpose of God's intention.

Faith can be perceived as a process. The challenge for some people is going through the process. Some people feel that going through a process is too much work. On the contrary, it is in the process—beginning with the seed or substance—where hope is used to further the development of purpose. Hebrew 11:1 says, "Now faith is the substance of things hoped for, the evidence of things not seen." When God chooses to give a person a gift or calling, He intends for it to serve a purpose for His glory. The gift or calling goes through a process of developing individuals for purpose. Proverbs 18:16-18 says, "A man's gift makes room for him, and brings him before great men." Faith in the process of developing individuals for purpose also acts as a tool in preparing others to receive their gift.

The process of discovering who God is as it relates to purpose gives life to who you are by faith. A few months ago, before my book *Worth the Struggle* was to be released, I shared with a coworker that my third published book would soon be available for purchase. Her response was, "OMG, I had no idea you like to write." My response to her was," I don't like to write; however, what I have is a passion to write." Usually when a gift chooses an individual, the gift is not something they merely like to do. There is a distinct difference in doing something you like and doing something you have a passion for. Passion is driven by instinct, which governs the gift God placed inside of you. Doing something you like is usually driven by feelings that you can easily shut off, turn on, or postpone until another time. Gifts from God cause people to work with great passion when faced with challenges that leave us with little control. Nevertheless, faith is the key or substance that controls everything we hope for. For some individuals, the process of living your life with purpose can be very challenging. However, the gift doesn't foster sorrow or repentance as part of the process of living out your purpose.

In the room where I do most of my writing, I wrote on the wall above my desk, "The Sweet Taste of Destiny Comes after the Burning and Stinging of the Anointing." In the process of living life with purpose, transformation at times is often dressed as adversities that can leave a scar. These adversities are necessary to help push people into purpose by changing their old thought processes to a mindset that thinks like Jesus. The gifts and callings from God come with burning and stinging of the anointing, but faith doesn't allow sorrow or regret to stay forever.

At the end of December 2019, many people believed that 2020 was the year of clear vision and a double blessing for their trouble. They expected a year where people would push on toward their destiny. In January 2020, the first confirmed case of COVID-19 was reported in the United States. It became an unexpected pandemic in the public eye and changed how the country and the world once viewed normal. Four months into the pandemic, the world as we once knew it had many questions such as how and why it was forced to live with COVID-19. By mid-May 2020, the world was aware that the deadly virus had a global death rate of more than 300,000, and more than 90,000 of them were people in the United States. The general public never saw this event coming. But it did arrive, and for some, it became an opportunity to see something hopeful come out of a devastating pandemic.

Surrounded by this hope, some people created unique, intimate moments with God through a personal relationship with Him by faith.

A CHANGED MINDSET

It takes faith to believe that something good could come out of COVID-19. God who is omnipresent and omniscient is using COVID-19 as a type of wrapping paper that is covering up something more powerful than the virus, even using the adverse ill effects for God's glory. Perhaps the underlying story of this pandemic and its adverse effects are how people see the peace of God in adversities. Our thought process—our mindset—controls our behavior and perception. Ephesians 1:18 says "the eyes of your understanding being enlightened; that you may know what is the hope of His calling, what are the riches of the glory of His inheritance in the saints." Adversities such as COVID-19 are opportunities for worshipers to acknowledge who God is by faith with the understanding that He is their hope in stable times as well as unstable times.

By August 2021, the world continued to struggle with COVID-19 and also the Delta variant, although vaccines and boosters were available in most countries for those who wanted it. A bigger challenge for people, especially in the United States, that appeared to be far more dangerous than the Delta variant or the threat of even another variant of COVID-19 was something as simple as caring for our neighbors by wearing a mask, standing six feet apart from others, and, if possible, getting vaccinated. The Pfizer, Moderna, and Johnson & Johnson vaccines have all become ineffective tools to fight the challenge of what is really the true virus that is making people spiritually and mentally sick. There is a sharp and deep separation among people, especially in the United States. I have never witnessed such a great division among states, religions, neighborhoods, families, communities, political associations, political parties, schools, local and global businesses, government officials, leaders, and parents, just to name a few.

The separation has divided people and built walls of anger among humanity. There is no common table where we can all sit down and work this out together and protect each other's back instead of building a fence that divides us. Could it be that COVID-19 is not just a threat to human lives physically but also a threat to our mindset and how we see ourselves and others?

And behold, a certain lawyer stood up and tested Him, saying, "Teacher, what shall I do to inherit eternal life?" He said to him, "What is written in the law? What is your reading of it?" So he answered and said, "'You shall love the LORD your God with all your heart, with all your soul, with all your strength, and with all your mind,' and 'your neighbor as yourself.'" And He said to him, "You have answered rightly; do this and you will live." But he, wanting to justify himself, said to Jesus, "And who is my neighbor?" Then Jesus answered and said: "A certain man went down from Jerusalem to Jericho, and fell among thieves, who stripped him of his clothing, wounded him, and departed, leaving him half dead. Now by chance a certain priest came down that road. And when he saw him, he passed by on the other side. Likewise a Levite, when he arrived at the place, came and looked, and passed by on the other side. But a certain Samaritan, as he journeyed, came where he was. And when he saw him, he had compassion. So he went to him and bandaged his wounds, pouring on oil and wine; and he set him on his own animal, brought him to an inn, and took care of him. On the next day, when he departed, he took out two denarii, gave them to the innkeeper, and said to him, 'Take care of him; and whatever more you spend, when I come again, I will repay you.' So which of these three do you think was neighbor to him who fell among the thieves?" And he said, "He who showed mercy on him." Then Jesus said to him, "Go and do likewise."

—Luke 10:25–37

COVID-19 is more than a virus that has proven to attack our physical health. It has attacked our mental health and, more importantly, how we treat our neighbor as the Good Samaritan did. It appears that the two largest platforms in the account of the Good Samaritan were people who justified their thought process according to their political or religious beliefs. The thought process in the United States as it relates to COVID-19 is like two people standing outside in the same spot, at the same time, at the same age, wearing the same clothes, and living in the same community. One person says it's raining outside with storm clouds, and the other says it's clear and sunny. That is a good example of the danger when a mindset has not been transformed and changed to think like Jesus Christ. Romans 12:2 says, "And do not be conformed to this world, but be transformed by the renewing of your mind, that you may prove what *is* that good and acceptable and perfect will of God."

COVID-19 can be perceived as a gift wrapped with deadly adverse effects. God is not only faithful during the adversity, but He is faithful to His Word regardless of the wrapping paper used to cover a gift. He is so faithful to His Word that He speaks the end before the beginning. The same level of standard as it relates to faith that God expects from people is the same level He holds for Himself. God finds great pleasure in His promises from His Word by faith. God looks for true worshippers. Moreover, His Word is our best example of how He should be worshipped. Isaiah 46:10 says, "Declaring the end from the beginning, and from ancient times *things* that are not yet done, saying, 'My counsel shall stand, and I will do all My pleasure.'" God is faithful in His intention to bring your purpose into fruition. God stands by His Word and everything He has spoken about your destiny, that it will come to pass in spite of any adversities you faced prior to reaching your purpose. "While the earth remains, seedtime and harvest, cold and heat, winter and summer, and day and night shall not cease" (Gen. 8:22).

In the course of developing purpose, it is a process like everything else in life. The role of worship in the process of seedtime and harvest, cold and heat, winter and summer, day and night is a way of acknowledging who God is in every season and circumstance. The walk in this process is done by faith and not with a mindset that looks to see a way to lessen the process or avoid the process. To worship God, one must do it in truth and in Spirit. God's Word is the truth, and knowing who God is recognizes that He is spirit, and it is by His spirit that He is revealed. "But God has revealed *them* to us through His Spirit. For the Spirit searches all things, yes, the deep things of God. For what man knows the things of a man except the spirit of the man which is in him? Even so no one knows the things of God except the Spirit of God" (1 Cor. 2:10-11). When gifts or callings from God choose you, don't be afraid because of uncertainty or disbelief, especially when the gift or calling is right in your face. *On the last day, that great day of the feast, Jesus stood and cried out, saying, "If anyone thirsts, let him come to Me and drink. He who believes in Me, as the Scripture has said, out of his heart will flow rivers of living water." But this He spoke concerning the Spirit, whom those believing in Him would receive; for the Holy Spirit was not yet given, because Jesus was not yet glorified.*—John 7:37-39

Jesus is a gift given to the world by God who is the living word and the substance of our faith. Romans 10:17 says, "So then faith cometh by hearing, and hearing by the word of God." Faith, which is the substance of who Jesus is, also is His inner core where He calls and places gifts in people according to God's purpose. His Word, which is Jesus, is a promise attached to all gifts or callings to help facilitate people in reaching their purpose. John 1:14 says, "And the Word became flesh and dwelt among us, and we beheld His glory, the glory as of the only begotten of the Father, full of grace and truth." Like gifts or callings, He also chose people according to His purpose. This same process that requires faith applies to those who are chosen. "But ye are a chosen generation, a royal priesthood, an holy nation, a peculiar people; that ye should shew forth the praises of him who hath called you out of darkness into his marvellous light" (1 Pet. 2:9 KJV).

Faith is not based on the amount of understanding people have from God pertaining to the gifts or callings. Needless to say, it is God who has chosen to give certain people gifts or callings, and faith is a vital component that supports their personal relationship with God. "But without faith it is impossible to please *Him*, for he who comes to God must believe that He is, and *that* He is a rewarder of those who diligently seek Him" (Heb. 11:6). "For I know the thoughts that I think toward you, says the Lord, thoughts of peace and not of evil, to give you a future and a hope" (Jer. 29:11).

A CHANGED MINDSET

However, there are moments in the process where God allows what appears to be evil to happen along the way to understanding why gifts or callings choose you. "But as for you, you meant evil against me; *but* God meant it for good, in order to bring it about as *it is* this day, to save many people alive" (Gen. 50:20). Not everyone will understand completely why the gift or calling chose them, but some will learn along the way as they develop their gift or calling in spite of the adversary or unforeseen adversities. "And we know that all things work together for good to them that love God, to them who are the called according to his purpose" (Rom. 8:28 KJV).

It is in the knowing or the core of who God is where faith becomes a way of thinking and not what is perceived through the natural eyes from a mindset that doesn't think like Jesus. "For we walk by faith, not by sight" (2 Cor. 5:7). To walk with God becomes a movement governed by faith where every step taken in this process empowers individuals to worship Him. As people worship Him, their faith becomes the framework to help shape who God is. "By faith we understand that the worlds were framed by the word of God, so that the things which are seen were not made of things which are visible" (Heb. 11:3).

John 1:1–5 says, "In the beginning was the Word, and the Word was with God, and the Word was God. He was in the beginning with God. All things were made through Him, and without Him nothing was made that was made. In Him was life, and the life was the light of men. And the light shines in the darkness, and the darkness did not comprehend it." There are times when followers become distracted with the steps in the process and don't see in their mindset that the substance of the process is where the focus should be. The substance of our faith is Jesus, and it is that same Word that God used to create. It is this faith that keeps it all together for the things that will come to fruition according to His plan.

Faith empowers people to become independent over things seen by the natural eye and a mindset that does not reflect Jesus. It is that same process that empowers others to believe. Opportunities or changes are created out of the substance of things hoped for and the evidence of things not seen.

In pursuit of purpose, a relationship in Jesus is a good beginning. Genesis 3:8–10 (KJV) says, "And they heard the voice of the Lord God walking in the garden in the cool of the day: and Adam and his wife hid themselves from the presence of the Lord God amongst the trees of the garden. And the Lord God called unto Adam and said unto him, Where art thou? And he said, I heard thy voice in the garden, and I was afraid, because I was naked; and I hid myself." Everyone who has a personal relationship with Jesus has an intimate Christmas story to tell. My Christmas story began when I heard Jesus say, "Althea, where are you?" In the Garden of Eden, Jesus walked on earth and asked Adam, "Where are you?" When He asked that, Jesus was stirring up in Adam's mind, his heart, and his spirit to think, "Where are you in relationship to Me?" John 10:27 says, "My sheep hear My voice, and I know them, and they follow Me." Like Adam, my Christmas story started with Jesus Christ asking me, "Where are you, Althea, in relationship to Me?"

God has used many people, places, and things as a channel to redirect them back to their first love, God the Almighty. It is by seeking first a relationship in Jesus as their Lord, Savior, and Redeemer. Park Street AME Zion Church in Peekskill, New York, was one of those places in the body of Christ where God drew me closer to Jesus rather than running away to hide from Him. This course of action of seeking a closer relationship with Jesus helped me know God as my Father and empowered me to worship Him as the great I AM. Five years ago, after receiving my doctorate degree in nursing, I drove to Peekskill to visit my parents. During my visit, I went to church with them and asked the pastor if I could give the church and my parents a gift of appreciation during the service.

The opportunity did arise, and I expressed my gratitude to Park Street AME Zion Church for being a facilitator in the plan of God for my life. I shared with the church that my parents lived a life of obedience to the Word of God and were my living examples of a type of Mary and Joseph in the 21st century. God allowed my mother to conceive me at the most inopportune time in the earlier part of their marriage. My mother was informed that she was expecting another child during her six-week checkup after giving birth to my brother. My birth was met with challenges and opposition. At Westchester Medical Center in Valhalla, New York, my mother entered an elevator on her way to the maternity ward and went into active labor. The only people in the elevator with her were a surgical orthodontist and his staff nurse. They called for help, but no one came to assist. The doctor and his nurse escorted my mother from the elevator to his office. I was born in the office of a surgical orthodontist where a shoestring from a tennis shoe was used to tie the umbilical cord until help finally arrived from the emergency department.

I began my education in the public school system, but my parents were forced to enroll me in a different school where I would be educated according to my learning disability—dyslexia. God instructed my parents to move me to a school in another town where people were not like me, to say the very least. I was instructed to wear a uniform to school. I was expected to speak, dress, act, and learn everything about their environment, even though the people in that environment rejected me merely because of the color of my skin. But my parents were faithful to God's Word and believed that what God had in store for me was greater than my feelings about how I was treated by other students and the faculty. Often God will give you a gift, and along with that gift will come hardship, pain, and questions. You may find yourself in hiding places while He is making room for your gift because the time has not come for its revelation to the world. To people who have been given a gift from God, don't be afraid of that gift. The day will come when the Giver of the gift will make room for it to be revealed to the world and for His glory. God's gifts are blessings, but they are often wrapped with adversities, challenges, hardships, and opposition. Christmas is revealed when the relationship with Jesus is something you seek first daily, regardless of the challenges you are forced to deal with. God demonstrated this type of love when He sent His Son Jesus to be persecuted and crucified on our behalf so we may have life and have it more abundantly. Perhaps the meaning of Christmas is the price you are willing to pay by going through the process of seeing the gift God gave you come to fruition.

Is it possible that the true meaning of celebrating Christmas is to unwrap the gift that lies within us? Because we went through the process of unwrapping the gift God gave us, we give Him two thumbs up to make room for it. "A man's gift maketh room for him, and bringeth him before great men" (Prov. 18:16 KJV).

I had a very lucrative job in the first part of 2021 during the COVID-19 pandemic, but I was laid off. I felt disappointed, but at the same time, I saw God making room for my gift by closing that door and having me use that time to write this book. Sometimes when God makes room for your gift, you may have to move out of your comfort zone and change your thought process in order to see His glory in your disappointments.

"Every branch in me that beareth not fruit he taketh away: and every branch that beareth fruit, he purgeth it, that it may bring forth more fruit" (John 15:2 KJV). There is a price we pay for every gift God gives us. But He empowers us with grace and mercy to pay the cost to purposely bear much fruit. The Christmas season we know today has Christmas trees, presents, and stories of Santa Claus, reindeer, and mistletoe. This mindset of how we see Christmas distracts from the mindset of seeking the God who is the source of those created things. Thinking like Jesus opens our thought processes to come to the realization that we need to seek after the One who created the stuff for the season and not seek after the stuff of the season that often captivates our mindset and dictates our behavior. Could it be that the real celebration of Christmas is to give birth to purpose? It starts by seeking the One who planted the desire in our heart that we can do all things in Christ Jesus. He is the One who speaks life over us that we were created *for* something and not just *from* something.

Chapter 3

"I CAN DO ALL THINGS"

Everything that facilitates our purpose is a scheduled court case for God to show up and win. Romans 8:28 reads, "And we know that all things work together for good to those who love God, to those who are the called according to *His* purpose." The mindset of the 21st century virgin doesn't perceive things as clearly as the mindset of the bride of Christ because her vision has not yet come to the clarity of perfection. As followers, we are being transformed into brides, one degree of glory to the next. While expecting abundance from God, there is a season of labor before delivery. Philippians 4:13 tells us, "I can do all things through Christ who strengthens me." His way is for His followers to obtain victory though His Word and to not totally depend on the system of the world. Jesus is asking us if we want to be made whole. In John 5:6 (NIV), we read, "When Jesus saw him lying there and learned that he had been in this condition for a long time, he asked him. 'Do you want to get well?'" We have to work with Jesus to decrease our sense of self and allow Him to increase within us. The next verses say, "The sick man answered Him, 'Sir, I have no man to put me into the pool when the water is stirred up; but while I am coming, another steps down before me.' Jesus said to him, 'Rise, take up your bed and walk.' And immediately the man was made well, took up his bed, and walked" (John 5:7–9).

A CHANGED MINDSET

It is very interesting to see how this man defended his illness and rationalized his condition. To him, it was his normal. Being crippled was painful for him, just as it would be getting up from a sick bed that you had been in for years. This man, like many followers, is faced with choices. However, one choice has proved to be uncomfortable and painful. The other choice, which can make him better, appears to be uncomfortable, painful, and impossible. In a follower's life, it is in moments such as these that faith has to override our perception of the what-ifs. The sick man's entire argument was based on his perception of his own limitations, and it would not let him be healed. Jesus was asking him if he was willing to let his perception of his limitation decrease and allow Him to increase in him. The discomfort would rise for a season, but true healing would come about. Jesus is not only greater than any challenge or disease, but He is also waiting to be sought after as the daily bread and water that sustains life for the living. God knows the pain that comes with disappointment and poor choices made in seeking first the kingdom of heaven.

After going through natural childbirth eight times, I have learned that God was never going to stop the labor process just because I was uncomfortable in the process. Jesus did not heal the invalid in the comfort of his bed. He told him to get up, pick up his mat, and walk. In spite of how uncomfortable it was for him initially to manage to stand to his feet, the Word of God proved to be faithful. Obedience plays a big and important role in the process of seeking the kingdom of God. Even though you may feel all alone and the pain appears to be unbearable, God is still there in all His glory. He is waiting and watching over your process, increasing your territory to make room for other promises to be manifested. These promises were placed inside you before you were born into this world and before any life situations became complicated or threatening. Jeremiah 1:5 says, "Before I formed you in the womb I knew you; before you were born I sanctified you; I ordained you a prophet to the nations."

There are stages of knowing your purpose as pregnant followers with destiny. These stages are often followed by seasons of feeling

"I CAN DO ALL THINGS"

overwhelmed by the pressure of your calling. Your parents brought you into the world, but it is God who predestined you to do something.

In his Word, God tells us that His people suffer from a lack of knowledge. Sin is the prime example of how things can be easily distorted and diverted from the truth. Jesus said that He came to give us life that we might have it abundantly. God's assessment of how we relate to Him has nothing to do with ability, race, age, wealth, social status, or gender. His kingdom is so different from what we perceive in life and is opened by a changed mindset that is like Jesus. Even though it is all around us, we cannot see the kingdom with our physical eyes or understand it with our human minds. God is omnipresent, and so is His kingdom.

> *But God hath revealed them unto us by his Spirit: For the Spirit searcheth all things, yea, the deep things of God. For what man knoweth the things of a man, save the spirit of man which is in him? Even so the things of God knoweth no man, but the Spirit of God. Now we have received, not the spirit of the world, but the Spirit which is of God; that we might know the things that are freely given to us of God.*
> —1 Cor. 2:10–12 KJV

God tells us in his Word to seek first the kingdom of heaven and its righteousness. We gain access to the kingdom of heaven through our hearts and minds while still living here on earth. The key to seeking the kingdom is to know Jesus personally as our Lord, to encourage our minds in the transformation. We have to search for God both with our minds and our hearts. Even if we can't understand Him, we should never give up. God promised that He would reward those who diligently seek after Him and see Him as a hidden treasure within themselves. In addition, He sent the power of the Holy Spirit to comfort us daily according to His purpose. As Matthew 6:11 (KJV) notes, "Give us this day our daily bread."

We don't need much faith to have the love of God. However, faith grows and develops from being exposed to situations that cause followers to trust God through difficulties. When Jesus was asleep in the boat on the Sea of Galilee in the midst of a storm, His followers were concerned because His response was not what they expected. Jesus questioned His followers' faith and willingness to open their eyes to the truth. Even though they had seen Him perform miracles, He had to prove to them again that their faith was already inside of them and not external. Part of having an intimate relationship with God is allowing Him to live inside you and assist you with the things that concern you externally and internally.

A master teaches an apprentice a certain skill. After the apprentice has mastered it, the next step is to take on their own apprentice. The ultimate expectation of a master is to teach their apprentice to become a master who empowers individuals to reach self-fulfillment. In my opinion, a savvy chess player is not someone who wins every match but rather someone who learns lessons from other chess players and looks for opportunities to teach others what they have learned. A master isn't concerned with the total number of wins or losses but rather teaching their skills to others to prepare them as game-changers. Matthew 4:19 (KJV) tells us, "And he saith unto them, Follow me, and I will make you fishers of men." The transformation from the mindset of the 21st century virgin to a bride of Christ can be likened to this process. The thought process of the bride of Christ empowers others to see Jesus as the way to the kingdom of God. "Then Jesus answered and said to them, 'Most assuredly, I say to you, the Son can do nothing of Himself, but what He sees the Father do; for whatever He does, the Son also does in like manner. For the Father loves the Son, and shows Him all things that He Himself does; and He will show Him greater works than these, that you may marvel'" (John 5:19–20).

We as followers are called to walk by faith and not by sight, and that faith comes from hearing the Word of God. John the Baptist represents the altar of salvation, just as Jesus represents the altar of the kingdom of heaven. John led the people to Jesus, and it is through Jesus that we enter the kingdom. Prayer is a form of worship that puts us in line with the will of the Father so it might be manifested. We pray to thank the Lord and give Him His due glory.

"I CAN DO ALL THINGS"

My heart sings praises to You, Lord. My tears are liquid joy that flow from my eyes and down my face. I thank You, Lord, for allowing me to be in Your presence. I thank You for allowing me to have the honor of sitting at Your feet. Thank You for answering every prayer, and thank You for seeing every tear so You have a record of the heartache and pain I felt growing up. Thank You for choosing me rather than having me choose You. Thank You for leaving me with the instruction to learn how to seek the kingdom of heaven first and its righteousness. Faith allows me to go boldly to Your merciful seat of grace with the assurance that You can do all things. You have created me in Your image and likeness that You may pour Your Spirit into me. You give me the power to tell a mountain to move, and it shall be done in Your name.

First Peter 1:21 says, "Who through Him believe in God, who raised Him from the dead and gave Him glory, so that your faith and hope are in God." Believing that all things from the natural world are our only source is not God's intention. He is the only source both naturally and supernaturally that allows resources to come into our possession. We do not want Christ to dwell among us in a limited or outdated form, but rather we want to seek Him in all things. It is only when we walk by faith that God becomes our walking stick of faith and, as a result, our vision and mobility. Christ encourages us to come to Him already knowing that He will reveal to us the things He has prepared for us.

God loves us as His children and instructs us to seek Him first and trust Him despite whatever we may see or feel otherwise. He wants us to have the same mind and heart that He has. It's like the centurion who requested that Jesus heal his servant by sending his word. We have to put aside what we see solely with our natural eyes and believe that God will implement His plan. Mary believed that through Jesus everyone could have life after death because He is the resurrection and the life. God is looking for His people to believe that He will reward those who work hard to find Him in their current thought process.

Jesus can bring life to any situation of death. "For the wages of sin *is* death, but the gift of God is eternal life in Christ Jesus our Lord" (Rom. 6:23). In fact, the more challenging a situation, the more God can radically act within it. Recently, I had some trouble with the toilet in my guest bathroom. When I flushed it, a great force of water sprang from the tank like a fire hydrant. Needless to say, I called the maintenance team and explained the situation. They told me to turn off the water until someone could come over to service it. With water everywhere at this point—from the bathroom to the dining room and flowing into the kitchen—I had to clean the floors while waiting for someone to come and fix the problem. Three days later, to my surprise, I noticed a three-inch mushroom growing from the bathroom floor. I was absolutely amazed as I never expected to see a mushroom growing on top of a floor in my bathroom inside an urban townhouse. That same week, I was feeling down as a result of my own struggle with sexual temptation. The message I received from God was that even in the midst of whatever mess I created or fell in, Jesus still saw me as His bride and wanted me to work on my relationship with Him. God, who is rich in grace and mercy, says that although we are dirty, through His Son we are made clean; and even in dirty places, God can call life to sprout forth in spite of the environment or complicated circumstances. God allowed plant life to grow in an unlikely environment of my bathroom floor. And He planted His Spirit in me although my lifestyle and mindset often wander after sinful activities. He placed rivers of living water to spring forth in a least likely person worth saving.

When waiting in the mess for our deliverance, we often limit God and don't look for Him to perform the impossible. Yet it is through the impossible that God reveals Himself to the true worshipper. He allows various obstacles to transform the 21st century virgin mindset into a mindset of a bride of Christ through adversities. We may not become holy overnight, but these lessons teach us about the renewal of our minds. The mind is a muscle that if not worked or exercised will fall into a state of disrepair. Zechariah 4:10 says, "For who has despised the day of small things?"

Journeying to the kingdom is not like going to Paris on holiday; it is the art of finding God in daily circumstances. When we acknowledge God, the keys to the kingdom are given to us. Everything we need as

"I CAN DO ALL THINGS"

followers is already within us; our only challenge is to discover that everything is already there through God, our source of power. The journey of faith requires both the capacity (space for the Holy Spirit) and ability (authority given by the Holy Spirit) to trust God and see him as our only source of life and hope.

Mark 8:34-35 says, "When He had called the people to *Himself*, with His disciples also, He said unto them, 'Whoever desires to come after Me, let him deny himself, and take up his cross, and follow Me. For whoever desires to save his life will lose it, but whoever loses his life for My sake and the gospel's will save it.'" In the process of understanding the steps that God has ordered, we must first seek Him. In Jesus lies the understanding of the substance of faith. The steps of the righteous person are ordered so they may learn to trust God. Even when we're faced with challenges, the Holy Spirit is part of the process and brings out the best in us. Now that's a real superhero! During these times of trial, God is teaching us through His Spirit to understand our reliance on Him.

> *My brethren, count it all joy when you fall into various trials, knowing that the testing of your faith produces patience. But let patience have its perfect work, that you may be perfect and complete, lacking nothing. If any of you lacks wisdom, let him ask of God, who gives to all liberally and without reproach, and it will be given to him. But let him ask in faith, with no doubting, for he who doubts is like a wave of the sea driven and tossed by the wind.*
> —James 1:2-6

God's lessons are not graded as pass or fail; they are available to you again and again until you have learned them. If you fail one time, He may send the lesson in a different form. It is the same lesson but through a different messenger. Trusting God's system comes about when spiritual life lessons are learned during your journey toward the kingdom of heaven. The essentials to seeking the kingdom are knowing God as your personal teacher and having faith that He will guide you. Motivation often lies in knowing that Jesus is the source of encouragement, growth, and maturity in seeking your destiny. When Jesus met the Samaritan woman at the well, He changed her life by giving her the living water of His Word. "Oh, taste and see that the Lord is good; blessed *is* the man *who* trusts in Him!" (Ps. 34:8).

God gives us each step in our lives as an ingredient to allow our destiny to come to fruition. When we understand this revelation, we appreciate each step more and more.

> *And at this* point *His disciples came, and they marveled that He talked with a woman; yet no one said, "What do You seek?" or, "Why are You talking with her?" The woman then left her waterpot, went her way into the city, and said to the men, "Come, see a Man who told me all things that I ever did. Could this be the Christ?" Then they went out of the city and came to Him. In the meantime His disciples urged Him, saying, "Rabbi, eat." But He said to them, "I have food to eat of which you do not know." Therefore the disciples said to one another, "Has anyone brought Him* anything *to eat?" Jesus said to them, "My food is to do the will of Him who sent Me, and to finish His work. Do you not say, 'There are still four months and* then *comes the harvest'? Behold, I say to you, lift up your eyes and look at the fields, for they are already white for harvest! And he who reaps receives wages, and gathers fruit for eternal life, that both he who sows and he who reaps may rejoice together. For in this the saying is true: 'One sows and another reaps.' I sent you to reap that for which you have not labored; others have labored, and you have entered into their labors."*
>
> —John 4:27–38

The Samaritan woman was chosen to stir the pot and encourage people to be fed by seeking Jesus. Many people were called that day to be with Jesus but not to fulfill that specific role. God does His best to work with what people consider lesser or not as important. God may call many people to seek Him, but only a few are chosen to perform certain tasks in the kingdom. Through seeking Him with a spiritual hunger, you are able to know and understand your purpose in the kingdom.

The steps the Lord has made are the journey, the process. Followers are tested along this journey to show what they are made of. Picture yourself walking in the rain and holding an umbrella. The rain represents the things life brings —both pleasant and unpleasant. The umbrella represents the day the Lord has made to cover and protect you. The umbrella is your Jehovah Jireh , Jehovah Nisse, Jehovah Raphe, Jehovah Raah, Jehovah Shammah, El Roi, El Shaddai, and all of His glorious names. Jesus is the cover we need for each day that He has made for you. God gives us each day as our daily bread, providing what we need to continue our journey. We must stay true to our steps and not be distracted from our purpose by the environment around us. Acknowledging that this is the day that the Lord has made is a form of worship, for it speaks to the circumstances that He has intentionally given us.

In the Lord's Prayer, Jesus instructs His followers to first acknowledge the kingdom. He also reminds us to receive our daily bread so that whatever the day brings, God provides what we need to match those challenges. Deuteronomy 33:25 tells us, "Your sandals *shall be* iron and bronze; as your days, *so shall* your strength *be*." Every day and every step God has ordered for His people is designed with the provisions we need. The bride of Christ understands this promise from God through her intimate relationship with Jesus. The 21st century virgin still struggles to understand how God thinks during times of adversity. She is called to leave purely religious activities behind and start to seek to love the One who loved her first.

Chapter 4

IT BEGINS AT GROUND ZERO

God loves the mindset of the 21st century virgin so much that He has a strategic plan to change that mindset to think like Christ Jesus. In Jeremiah 29:11, God tells us, "For I know the thoughts that I think toward you, says the LORD, thoughts of peace and not of evil, to give you a future and a hope." However, what some followers fail to see is God's thought process and what He already knows before transforming and changing a mindset to think like a bride of Christ Jesus.

In the process of discovering your true identity, the mindset of the 21st century virgin becomes disenchanted at times with past circumstances. This thought process in the 21st century virgin will hinder you from moving toward your destiny, similar to the five foolish virgins. "Listen to this, O Job; stand still and consider the wondrous works of God" (Job 37:14). As the mindset of the 21st century virgin becomes a better worshipper, she begins to appreciate not only who God is but also how He controls the transformation process. In Matthew 7:13–14, we read, "Enter by the narrow gate; for wide *is* the gate and broad *is* the way that leads to destruction, and there are many who go in by it. Because narrow *is* the gate and difficult *is* the way which leads to life, and there are few who find it."

Followers who seek the kingdom of heaven will come to know that they are on a unique journey to discover God through a personal relationship with Christ. Many people have a broad view of life that enables them to enter into a common way of seeing and understanding society. Jesus spoke to the people again in parables, saying this:

> *The kingdom of heaven is like a certain king who arranged a marriage for his son, and sent out his servants to call those who were invited to the wedding; and they were not willing to come. Again, he sent out other servants, saying, "Tell those who are invited, 'See, I have prepared my dinner; my oxen and fatted cattle* are *killed, and all things* are *ready. Come to the wedding.'" But they made light of it and went their ways, one to his own farm, another to his business. And the rest seized his servants, treated* them *spitefully, and killed* them. *But when the king heard about it, he was furious. And he sent out his armies, destroyed those murderers, and burned up their city. Then he said to his servants, "The wedding is ready, but those who were invited were not worthy. Therefore go into the highways, and as many as you find, invite to the wedding." So those servants went out into the highways and gathered together all whom they found, both bad and good. And the wedding hall was filled with guests. But when the king came in to see the guests, he saw a man there who did not have on a wedding garment. So he said to him, "Friend, how did you come in here without a wedding garment?" And he was speechless. Then the king said to the servants, "Bind him hand and foot, take him away, and cast* him *into outer darkness; there will be weeping and gnashing of teeth." For many are called, but few* are *chosen.*
>
> —Matt. 22:2–14

IT BEGINS AT GROUND ZERO

God is sending out servants to gather up people who may be viewed by society as the least likely to be on a wedding invitation list. Regardless of their past or present relationship with Him, they are invited because of His grace and their willingness to be open to it and come. Religious followers may see these people as unworthy of an invitation and may regard the guests as least likely to have been chosen by the King. However, these guests are the ones God is seeking a relationship with. As His servants, we are not the way, but we have Jesus, who is the way.

The journey in seeking God is so unlike any other journey we take. It is a journey that requires the fruit of the Spirit. It is impossible to undertake this journey alone, but God, who is rich in mercy, is there to lead us on the way. The promise and the pressure are paired together. The only way to complete the task is to know that the Holy Spirit is inside of us and is in control of our destinies. If we seek the kingdom, everything we need will fall into place. All of heaven and earth await Jesus so they may be transformed, discover their purpose, and give birth to God's promise for them. Seeking the kingdom of God takes work. It is so much more than going to church once or twice a week and passively listening to a preacher. Too often as followers, we don't want to start with God at ground zero and empty ourselves to His will for us. If we could seek God as our Creator instead of just seeking the things He has created, how much better prepared we would be to see and worship Him.

"And the light shineth in the darkness; and the darkness comprehended it not" (John 1:5 KJV). God tells His children to let the mind of Christ be in them. Having His mind fosters an appreciation for the thoughts of God. In addition, it places us as followers in the position to be anxious about nothing and engage in true prayer and thanksgiving. "'I am the Alpha and the Omega, *the* Beginning and *the* End,' says the Lord, 'who is and who was and who is to come, the Almighty'" (Rev. 1:8). God requires us to give Him our all. He doesn't want us to focus only on the parts of us we believe belong to Him. Being a cheerful giver is a great first step toward surrendering to Him. As we become more mature in our walk and personally interact with Jesus, we will discover that our service to others reflects our relationship with Him. Abraham

A CHANGED MINDSET

offered Isaac up as a sacrifice to God because He commanded from him an offering. However, the faith Abraham had in God's commands rescued Isaac, proving that obedience outweighs sacrifice.

God is so awesome in His giving, but when we tithe, we give God 10 percent of our gross net. Tithing is giving God a portion of the boundless love He has given us, because in reality, 100 percent belongs to Him. My intimate relationship with God through Jesus fosters and perfects my worship, which further empowers my faith. I can never beat God's giving, but God is not looking for material things as a return of gratitude. Rather, He is looking for 100 percent of the things that capture our attention and hearts. God wants to ultimately transform His people to believe that He is God over everything. Tithing the full 10 percent or more leads us to obedience, not sacrifice. Through this process, our relationship grows into our giving back to God a worthy offering that reflects a relationship of trust, not what's in our wallets. Unfortunately, there are people who believe they are doing God a favor by tithing. However, it is God who is providing us His favor by giving us greater gifts that money can't buy. Understanding this concept allows us to give more cheerfully. It's not the money that concerns God; it is where our hearts are in the giving.

The fruit of the Spirit is the evidence that God has taken up residence within you. Galatians 5:22–23 states, "But the fruit of the Spirit is love, joy, peace, longsuffering, kindness, goodness, faithfulness, gentleness, self-control." When you become a new creature in Christ Jesus, you are learning to bear the fruit of the Spirit. Do not be surprised if God requires you to demonstrate kindness or patience with someone on a whole new level than what you have been accustomed to. That can be challenging, but having the mentality that all things belong to God and that He is the source of all will help you become a more cheerful giver of the fruit of the Spirit.

> *Now both Jesus and His disciples were invited to the wedding. And when they ran out of wine, the mother of Jesus said to Him, "They have no wine." Jesus said to her, "Wom-*

an, what does your concern have to do with Me? My hour has not yet come." His mother said to the servants, "Whatever He says to you, do it." Now there were set there six waterpots of stone, according to the manner of purification of the Jews, containing twenty or thirty gallons apiece. Jesus said to them, "Fill the waterpots with water." And they filled them up to the brim. And He said to them, "Draw some out now, and take it to the master of the feast." And they took it. When the master of the feast had tasted the water that was made wine, and did not know where it came from (but the servants who had drawn the water knew), the master of the feast called the bridegroom. And he said to him, "Every man at the beginning sets out the good wine, and when the guests have well drunk, then the inferior. You have kept the good wine until now!" This beginning of signs Jesus did in Cana of Galilee, and manifested His glory; and His disciples believed in Him.

—John 2:2–11

Jesus's mother must have said, "Yes, amen," to Him as the author and finisher of her faith. Her faith pushed Him to turn the water into wine even after He told her that His time had not yet come. How did his mother, Mary, move Jesus to perform this miracle? What did she say to Him that moved Him so? Did she remind Him of His Word, which fostered her belief and faith in God? Mary was empowered by the Holy Spirit to ask Jesus to help the newlyweds and instruct the servants to follow every word that came from the lips of Jesus. Somewhere in her relationship with God, she had entered the inner court of faith. In the inner court, there is no limit to what God can do. When Mary had been informed she was pregnant with Jesus, she had said, "Let it be to me according to your word," and she received the Holy Spirit. Mary was at an age where her body was able to conceive, but getting pregnant was not part of her plan as she prepared to marry Joseph. The Holy Spirit impregnated her when she gave up her own will for God's will. Her previous experience with the Lord empowered her to approach Jesus at the wedding. By being previously exposed to the rhythm of God, she was able to understand His timing and help bring about His plan. Through the Holy Spirit and her faith in God, Mary was moved to say yes to God, and Jesus was able to turn water into wine.

There is power in the will of the Father, and it is manifested when it works alongside our own ability to match Jesus's rhythm or mindset. The miracle of the wine shows us what is possible when Jesus shows up. The lesson is not in the miracle itself but in what is behind it. Faith was required to move Jesus to perform the miracle, and it is required to bring who He is at His core into our lives. By faith Mary acted, and Jesus was able to perform the miracle because Mary believed in who He is at His core. Faith is activated every time we worship God. His mother, the woman at the well, the woman with the blood disorder, the centurion who had a beloved servant near death, the woman whose daughter was possessed, and the man with leprosy who returned to thank Jesus for His healing and miracle—these six people saw Jesus for who He is at His core. In return, Jesus's interactions with them far exceeded their expectations. Mary demonstrated compassion toward a bride and a groom at a wedding in Cana of Galilee, and the woman living with a 12-year blood disorder looked up to Jesus to be made whole. They all were empowered by God's grace and moved by His Spirit. What was going on in the minds and hearts of Mary and the woman with the blood disorder to enable these miracles to happen? The answer is that they believed that God would provide something greater than what they had already been given or experienced in the past. These two women made up their minds to press through the crowd and use their faith in God to do the impossible. Against all odds, the Holy Spirit kept them connected to their faith in God.

We see in these two women living with difficult challenges how faith without works is dead. They, like many other people of God, shared similar struggles and were able to overcome them through their extraordinary faith in who Jesus is at His core. When Mary sought help from her Son, she was seeking help from God Himself. She came to Jesus knowing who He was, not based solely on her mother-son relationship with Him. Just imagine if Mary had allowed her own human perception to govern her actions and not recognize Jesus for who He is. The wedding at Cana was not the time for Jesus to make wine, but rather it was the time for God's people to understand the power of faith behind the miracle. The guests were able to acknowledge how good the new wine was, and they most likely remembered it for the rest of their lives. Perhaps Mary's mindset was to focus on the revelation of her Lord rather than the recognition of her Lord. The wedding party ran out of wine, yet Jesus proclaimed to His mother that His time had not yet come. Mary, who saw the need anyway, decided to intercede on behalf of the wedding party. God used this opportunity to demonstrate mercy and grace to the bride and groom, who represent the church and Christ. Perhaps the wine represents that grace and mercy.

Each day we have is another day God has given us to make things right with Him. Moreover, the celebration of the second coming of Christ will be the time for Him to be united with His bride. The wine at the Last Supper was the blood of Christ shed on the cross. And when Jesus died and was resurrected from the grave, He gave us the wine of eternal life. Mary may have initiated the turning of the water into wine at the wedding feast as a foreshadowing of the wine of salvation present at the Last Supper. "But if we walk in the light as He is in the light, we have fellowship with one another, and the blood of Jesus Christ His Son cleanses us from all sin" (1 John 1:7). What is it that dwells within us that makes us love Jesus and desire to worship God? What is it that makes us stand up to adversity? What motivates us to run and tell the world the good news of what Jesus has done? We learn from Mary to believe in the Word of God and allow it to create faith in us. We all have the power to obtain all things through the love of God if we are called according to His purpose. The blood of Jesus cleanses us and gives us eternal life, and the Holy Spirit makes us holy and acceptable to God, allowing us to worship Him as Jehovah-Mekoddishkem, the Lord who sanctifies you.

Chapter 5

SET UP FOR A COMEBACK

Sometimes my first reaction toward disappointment is a feeling of loneliness and annoyance. During these moments, my vision of God usually becomes distorted. When I feel like I've failed, I find myself easily becoming angry with God and myself. Often in these situations, I ask myself, "Why would God allow me to fail a test after I prepared myself for it?" Of course, in these instances, I'm depending on God more as a magic genie than a Father who sees purpose even in my disappointments.

Many times in life human failures look very different through the eyes of God than how we see them. God's thoughts, of course, are not our thoughts. I used to believe that a good education and hard work with a healthy dose of ambition and determination were enough to be successful in anything. But God's vision and plan for me are so much bigger than my own intentions. Often I have to decrease my self-righteousness to provide permission for Jesus to increase within me. This process, though, can be uncomfortable and discouraging. However, for followers, it becomes a birthing room for the mindset of the bride of Christ. It reminds me of labor pains during childbirth; when it's all over, the sense of joy is overwhelming as the fruits of our labor are laid in our arms. God knows the pain and the hurt that come with your disappointments, but He is not going to stop the process of pain during

A CHANGED MINDSET

your transformation any more than you would stop the labor to avoid having pain. Labor and pain are dependent on one another to effectively produce fruit.

Several stages in the birthing process are similar to the stages in the transformation of the mindset of the 21st century virgin to the mindset of the bride of Christ. After you have passed through the transition stage and are fully dilated, the doorway to the birth canal is fully open. When God positions you to give birth to your potential, you are going to have to push. It will be uncomfortable, but only for a season. With the mindset of the bride of Christ, you have the strength to keep pushing from a deep place in your belly where His living rivers of waters are moving. The pain or discomfort you feel stems from the process of coming into your purpose. God is your coach, cheering you on and encouraging you as the process of actualizing your purpose is completed. Each time you complete a new level of growth, you realize that everything does indeed work out for your good and to God's glory. The final outcome you are journeying toward is actually a comeback, a transition from a 21st century virgin mindset to understanding your purpose as the bride of Christ.

In God's vocabulary, there are no terms such as learning disabilities, racial differences, pass or fail, or too late or too old. God's world is so different from ours; His Kingdom is near us, around us, and inside of us. As his children, we may not understand it now, but we are invited to live in the kingdom daily by knowing who God is. Needless to say, the kingdom of God becomes more concrete and less abstract to those with a changed mindset. The more God lives and has His being in our thought process, the more the kingdom of God and His righteousness become an attainable reality. The kingdom of God is not accessible to us through our natural state; however, the Holy Spirit can remove the foreskin from our spiritual hearts so we may understand the process of seeking the kingdom here on earth. This journey starts with a personal relationship with Jesus through whom we become new creatures, and all things are made new. Likewise, the Holy Spirit teaches us to pray as we ought, which is with God rather than to God.

SET UP FOR A COMEBACK

John 3:30 says, "He must increase, but I *must* decrease." Each time God corrects me, part of me dies, but through that death, new life begins to take its rightful place. A seed, in its due time, brings forth a harvest. The concepts of seed, time, and harvest are similar to the transformation to a triumphant comeback for a changed mindset in Christ. I am made whole and am complete in Him. Sometimes Jesus will say no in order to say yes to something much better than what you can see with your eyes. His no is a yes to something much better farther down the road. Jesus once told a story about how a shepherd left his 99 sheep to go after the one that strayed. This is a metaphor for how valuable every soul is to God. A set is not complete until every piece has been gathered. And the overall value of the whole is decreased if every piece is not in its proper place. The lost one is so important to God that He created a plan to bring the lost sheep back to His fold. "And when he has found *it*, he lays it on his shoulders, rejoicing. And when he comes home, he calls together *his* friends and neighbors, saying to them, 'Rejoice with me, for I have found my sheep which was lost!' I say to you that likewise there will be more joy in heaven over one sinner who repents than over ninety-nine just persons who need no repentance'" (Luke 15:5-7).

Our reunion with God is the reason Christ was sent. Jesus came so the mindset of the 21st century virgin could be transformed into the mindset of His bride. "Now no chastening seems to be joyful for the present, but painful; nevertheless, afterward it yields the peaceable fruit of righteousness to those who have been trained by it" (Heb. 12:11). God has prepared a fabulous transformation for the 21st century virgin to be His bride, empowered and no longer a slave to religious activity. However, the transformation begins with a changed mindset, motivated by conviction and led with chastening. Romans 12:2 tells us that we need to renew our minds. Some people tend to stop seeking God when they have received salvation. In doing so, they limit themselves in fulfilling their purpose. That is similar to the concept of putting down your nets to follow Jesus. You may not be able to choose your challenges, but you can choose to glorify God through them.

A CHANGED MINDSET

God is setting things in motion for my transformation, even when I feel He has not answered my prayers. As followers, we too often tend to wish that God would change our challenges based on the strength we have to overcome them. But God has strategically created challenges for us where we learn from His present, perfect peace, regardless of the level of difficulty. His peace doesn't always change the situation, but His peace will always change how we think or see the situation. His mindset will empower us to go through challenging situations that would normally provoke uncertainty. Often it is those challenges that bring negativity, unwarranted stressors, and increased feelings of anxiety.

God wants us to acknowledge Him before trouble comes. In doing so, He teaches us how to worship Him and thank him daily for the day He has made. When trouble does come, we don't have to search for Him because we already have the knowledge that He is omnipresent. *Be careful for nothing; but in everything by prayer and supplication with thanksgiving let your requests be made known unto God. And the peace of God, which passeth all understanding, shall keep your hearts and minds through Christ Jesus. Finally, brethren, whatsoever things are true, whatsoever things are honest, whatsoever things are just, whatsoever things are pure, whatsoever things are lovely, whatsoever things are of good report; if there be any virtue, and if there be any praise, think on these things.* —Phil. 4:6–8 KJV

As followers take on the mindset of the bride of Christ, their ability to manage conflict increases. "For unto whomsoever much is given, of him shall be much required: and to whom men have committed much, of him they will ask the more" (Luke 12:48 KJV). God knows what you can manage and will increase your territory to bless you. The strength to manage conflict is proven not through unforgiveness but through forgiveness. As you walk with God daily, He will groom you by placing people and situations in your path that will allow you to exercise the muscle of forgiveness. Every day, the world presents us with choices. Our response or reaction to those choices is totally dependent on whether we have the 21st century virgin mindset or the mindset of the bride of Christ. It is that type of thought process that places followers for a comeback. In Numbers 13:30 (NIV), Caleb gives a report to Moses. "Then Caleb silenced the people before Moses and said, 'We should go up and take possession of the land, for we can certainly do it.'" God is looking to His elect to give Him a good report of the possibilities and not just how our enemy appears to be so much bigger or more numerous than we are. God, through Caleb, is telling us that our job is to believe that He is God.

The mindset of the 21st century virgin does not have a personal, intimate relationship with Christ, and as a result, the outcome is not always set for a great comeback. God tests your faith in Him to see if you really believe He is God. The next time you are faced with a challenge and your back is against the wall, try believing that the God you serve is greater than what you perceive as difficult challenges. The mindset of the 21st century virgin reacts to challenges and adversities, whereas the mindset of the bride of Christ responds to those things. Faith perfectly aligns the bride of Christ in a walk with God and not a walk based on our understanding of what we see.

Chapter 6

FAITH IS A DIFFERENT PAIR OF LENSES

The Lord God taught me how to walk by faith and not by sight through the example of losing a pair of contact lenses in my bathroom. I began my morning by getting ready to put my contacts in, but this time I had forgotten the top was already loose before shaking it to clean the lenses. Every drop of the solution as well as the lenses went flying. I began to look for my contact lenses in spite of the small chance I had of finding them. I remembered the lesson that sometimes we find the Word of God in the least likely of places and decided to apply it to my search. Even when I deviated from this plan, His voice kept reminding me to keep looking in the least expected places. After searching for a while, I caught site of a large bottle of antiseptic mouthwash on a ledge, away from the general mess of the bathroom. Upon taking a closer look, I saw that both contact lenses had landed right on the word *Antiseptic*. This unexpected event was part of God's strategic lesson for me to learn that I am to walk by faith and not by fear. Although fear and doubt will always be hanging around faith, we must choose to walk by faith and not allow fear and doubt to take control of how we walk. The mindset of the bride of Christ has an intimate relationship with Jesus; however, there are times when we need to catch ourselves when we allow fear to take our faith hostage.

When we seek to recognize Jesus, we often can't trace Him. To find Him, we must worship Him in truth and by His Spirit. In Psalm 100, we learn that we need to enter into His gates with thanksgiving and into His courts with praise. In Hebrews 11:6 (KJV) we read, "But without faith it is impossible to please him: for him that cometh to God must believe that he is, and that he is a rewarded of them that diligently seek him." We have to stop trying to control God's methodology and mode of operation. It is only in the name of Jesus that things are changed. In Romans 15:13 (KJV) we read, "Now the God of hope fill you with all joy and peace in believing, that ye may abound in hope, through the power of the Holy Ghost." Just as Mary was filled with the Holy Spirit, we are filled with the same Spirit and are empowered by His Word. "And the Lord said unto Moses, I have seen this people, and, behold, it is a stiffnecked people: Now therefore let me alone, that my wrath may wax hot against them, and that I may consume them: and I will make of thee a great nation. And the Lord relented from the evil which he thought to do unto his people" (Exod. 32:9–10, 14 KJV).

First Corinthians 2:9 (KJV) states, "But as it is written, eye hath not seen, nor ear heard, neither have entered into the heart of man, the things which God hath prepared for them that love him." God expects you to transform your own way of thinking and change with a new thought process, a mindset like Christ's. I learned this lesson when I was two weeks into my master of science in nursing program. My professor gave me feedback on a written assignment I had submitted, and I felt the way she graded the assignment was too harsh and that her expectations were too high for someone who had just gotten a bachelor of science in nursing degree four months before. When I told this to my professor, her response was, "I expect you to write as a scholar when submitting assignments in this program." I told my daughters that my professor's request was unrealistic because I was not a scholar and it was only my first semester. In my last week of classes, God revealed to me that He has similar high expectations of me. As His children, it is vital that we

FAITH IS A DIFFERENT PAIR OF LENSES

change the way we think. I had to change my thinking process and see myself through my teacher's eyes and, more importantly, through the eyes of God. Our destiny will be revealed as our relationship with Jesus further develops. We have to stop trying to find our identity in what we perceive as limitations or the ideologies of this world and find it through the thoughts of God.

The woman with the alabaster box of ointment found God's plan and purpose for her life and celebrated that God was in her life. "And [she] stood at his feet behind him weeping, and began to wash his feet with tears, and did wipe them with the hairs of her head, and kissed his feet, and anointed them with the ointment" (Luke 7:38 KJV). In another example in Luke 17:15-16 (KJV), we read, "And one of them, when he saw that he was healed, turned back, and with a loud voice glorified God, and fell down on his face at his feet, giving him thanks: and he was a Samaritan." The woman with the alabaster box and one of the 10 healed lepers both thanked Jesus for what He had done for them. But this expression of thankfulness was secondary to their deep and unspoken connection with Jesus. After a transformation like that, you can see Jesus for who He is—the Lord who sanctifies you. At that point, you are able to move from the outer courts to the inner courts.

Jesus is waiting for His people to turn around and come into the inner court through the confession of their sins. Jesus is waiting to wash away our sins and dress us in the wedding gown of his grace so we may join Him in holy marriage.

Lord, thank You for fostering within me the ability to worship You by revealing to me how much You love me and how powerful Your love is for me. Because You are God, you have ordained Your followers to be created in Your image. I am a spirit with natural experiences to live with purpose and for Your glory. You have instilled in me everything I need to be victorious, and You have helped me conquer those things that were formed against me in meeting Your purpose. Lord, thank You for sending Your Son to take my place as a sacrifice. Because of who Jesus is, I have an alabaster box of ointment to give for Your glory. Thank You for giving me something that is worthy to give back to You.

A CHANGED MINDSET

When Jesus was a young boy traveling with his family, He decided to stay back in the city of Jerusalem while His family started the trip back home. His mother did not realize until a few days into the journey that her son was not with them. She had to return to Jerusalem, most likely feeling very frantic while seeking Jesus. Like Mary, we as followers need to seek the kingdom of heaven frantically until we find Jesus within us. Once the Word of God begins to take root in your heart, the kingdom becomes more accessible and is no longer a mystery. When you are operating under the influence of the Holy Spirit, you can expect transformation and change. "Sanctify yourselves therefore, and be ye holy: for I am the LORD your God. And ye shall keep my statutes, and do them: I am the LORD which sanctify you" (Lev. 20:7–8 KJV).

> *Then He said to him, "A certain man gave a great supper and invited many, and sent his servant at supper time to say to those who were invited, 'Come, for all things are now ready.' But they all with one accord began to make excuses. The first said to him, 'I have bought a piece of ground, and I must go and see it. I ask you to have me excused.' And another said, 'I have bought five yoke of oxen, and I am going to test them. I ask you to have me excused.' Still another said, 'I have married a wife, and therefore I cannot come.' So that servant came and reported these things to his master. Then the master of the house, being angry, said to his servant, 'Go out quickly into the streets and lanes of the city, and bring in here the poor and the maimed and the lame and the blind.' And the servant said, 'Master, it is done as you commanded, and still there is room.' Then the master said to the servant, 'Go out into the highways and hedges, and compel them to come in, that my house may be filled. For I say to you that none of those men who were invited shall taste my supper.'"*
>
> —Luke 14:16-24

FAITH IS A DIFFERENT PAIR OF LENSES

Salt is good, but what good is it if it loses its flavor or purpose? God has given you everything you need to be all He has called you to be. He has given you all the ingredients and tools you need to prepare the meal you were instructed to prepare. When Jesus reveals Himself to you, He is also revealing to you the things you need to get the job done. God has given me the grace and mercy to write down the words you are reading now. I am only a conduit for His words and just a tool to do the work of the Lord. So when I am not sure what to do next, God reminds me, "Daughter, what does my Word say? Read it back to me!" God loves to hear His Word read back to Him. If we find ourselves in a tight place and are not sure what the next step may be, we may have become distracted from the One who called us to the assignment. God responds more quickly to His own Word than to our pity parties, fears, or doubts. All of us like to feel sorry for ourselves at times, which is why we need salvation. Through our worship of God, we are able to demonstrate not what we know but the strength of our faith. We learn that waiting on God is a form of worship, and through this waiting, we are declaring that the Lord will renew our strength. When we wait on the Lord, we are demonstrating to others that God is a problem-solver and a promise-keeper. Waiting on God is acknowledging that we are willing to do what God has been waiting on us to do. Because God is omniscient, He is the One who is always waiting on us; we are not waiting on Him.

> *Then shall the kingdom of heaven be likened unto ten virgins, which took their lamps, and went forth to meet the bridegroom. And five of them were wise, and five were foolish. They that were foolish took their lamps, and took no oil with them: but the wise took oil in their vessels with their lamps. While the bridegroom tarried, they all slumbered and slept. And at midnight there was a cry made, Behold, the bridegroom cometh; go ye out to meet him. Then all those virgins arose, and trimmed their lamps. And the foolish said unto the wise, Give us of your oil; for our lamps are gone out. But the wise answered, saying, Not so; lest there*

> *be not enough for us and you: but go ye rather to them that sell, and buy for yourselves. And while they went to buy, the bridegroom came; and they that were ready went in with him to the marriage: and the door was shut. Afterward came also the other virgins, saying, Lord, Lord, open to us. But he answered and said, Verily I say unto you, I know you not. Watch therefore, for ye know neither the day nor the hour wherein the Son of man cometh.*
> —Matt. 25:1–13 KJV

The blessing of the Lord is in the waiting process. Obedience helps followers learn how to love the waiting process. It is through the waiting process that Jesus reveals Himself to the mindset of His bride. Every virgin in the parable we read understood that the waiting process prepares them for God. Therefore, the waiting process from a mindset of the 21st century virgin to the mindset of the bride of Christ Jesus is necessary in order for change to take place in the process.

The tree that brings forth fruit is a blessing to many. Trees, however, cannot produce other trees without seeds. Your true increase is not on the things you ask of God but in the seeds of faith that activate your love toward Him. In seeking Him rather than things, you will find everything. If you keep your mind focused on Him, He will grant you perfect peace. There are so many ways to worship God. Worshippers are learners who demonstrate what they have learned through their worship. They love to seek not after the solution to their problems but after the understanding of the One who has set all things in order. When you seek Him, you will find everything you need. If you keep your mind on Him, He will grant you perfect peace. Christ demonstrated discipline and submission to the will of the Father and showed how a prophet is often not welcome in his native land. But as you grow in your worship, you will learn to bless those who curse you and pray for those who use you. The mighty hand of God allows your enemies to harass you so you can learn about His power and strength. God uses your enemies to help build up your character. That is one reason it is so important to pray for your enemies.

FAITH IS A DIFFERENT PAIR OF LENSES

They don't know what they're doing and how God is still using them as part of His plan to shape you for His use.

Jesus takes our life's challenges as He did for the woman with the alabaster box and transforms them, washing away our sins. Only God's solvent can pay the price for our sins and the debt we owed from them. His solvent is love, and we are called to use it to break down all barriers that stand between us and His plan. Through the power of the Holy Spirit, every situation can be transformed and changed to our advantage. The Lord is very creative and will use your enemies as a stool for you to stand on to reach something God wants you to have.

I cannot emphasize enough that this battle between you and your enemies is not really about you. The Lord knows what He is doing, and we need to stay out of it. When you pray, say to the Lord, in your own words, how you need to stop making excuses and let God work in your life. Because we have the name of Jesus, we have power through Him to be change agents and complete our assigned mission, even if it seems impossible to complete. As children of God, we can tell Him that we will complete our journey to our purpose, no matter how challenging it is. Romans 15:13 (KJV) tells us, "Now the God of hope fill you with all joy and peace in believing, that ye may abound in hope, through the power of the Holy Ghost." God wants us to speak His Word over impossible and complicated situations and believe not just that He can solve them but that He will solve them by the power of His Spirit living in us.

Getting to the real you and understanding your true identity is a process that begins with seeking the kingdom of God. This process is a journey that starts with a seed. The purpose of the seed is to keep your focus on what to hope for from God although we don't know what it will look like under the substance where the seed has been buried. Seeking the kingdom of God takes a life journey, and it starts by having faith as small as a mustard seed. The purpose of the seed is much smaller than it appears to the naked eye, but it can move mountains. Hope is the driving power of faith that is used to develop the seed into an apple. In turn, the apple will produce more seeds, and the cycle continues as more people come to know God who lives, moves, and gives them purpose.

A CHANGED MINDSET

Jeremiah 1:5 (KJV) teaches us, "Before I formed thee in the belly I knew thee; and before thou camest forth out of the womb I sanctified thee, and I ordained thee a prophet unto the nations." One of the many glories of God is that He sees His people as complete. Before your mother gave birth to you, God had already created you and decreed who you were to be. When creating a work of art, an artist sees the final piece in their mind before it becomes a reality, despite the surrounding mess. God is faithful to His Word and is slow to anger because He sees the end result from the beginning. Getting to know God can be a seemingly messy process; however, the steps of the righteous person are ordered, and God remains in control. In the chaos, you will discover the seeds of greatness. "And we know that all things work together for good to them that love God, to them who are the called according to his purpose" (Rom. 8:28 KJV).

> *Now when He got into a boat, His disciples followed Him. And suddenly a great tempest arose on the sea, so that the boat was covered with the waves. But He was asleep. Then His disciples came to* Him *and awoke Him, saying, "Lord, save us! We are perishing!" But He said to them, "Why are you fearful, O you of little faith?" Then He arose and rebuked the winds and the sea, and there was a great calm. So the men marveled, saying, "Who can this be, that even the winds and the sea obey Him?"*
> —Matt. 8:23–27

Too often followers find a situation where they are looking for Jesus to react or make a power move when they see themselves confronted with challenging situations or dangerous adversities. This is based on the way they think and their perception of what they see. In this type of mindset, followers become limited in seeing Jesus for who He is. The followers in this story could not understand why and how Jesus was able to rest in the midst of a storm. They were fighting to stay alive in the same boat where they found Jesus asleep. Their natural eyes could not expose Jesus as One who had control over what was fighting them.

FAITH IS A DIFFERENT PAIR OF LENSES

However, faith was the eyes they needed to see it was their lack of faith in who Jesus was, even in the midst of a dangerous storm. Jesus allowed Himself to fall asleep, knowing a storm would frighten them to think they were at death's door. He used this opportunity to demonstrate to them that things they fear are subject to His authority. "Be still, and know that I *am* God; I will be exalted among the nations, I will be exalted in the earth!" (Ps. 46:10).

God wants people to see Him as far greater than any uncertainty. The core of Jesus is the substance of what faith is. The substance of faith supports having a loyal, intimate personal relationship with God. Jesus often questioned the faith of others as He redirected their mindset toward building a deeper personal, loyal relationship with God. "So then faith *comes* by hearing, and hearing by the word of God" (Rom. 10:17). It is this type of relationship with God that supports intimate moments with Him and strengthens our faith and loyalty to Him. Loyalty to God is better developed among people when they are faced with adversities. It is in these moments that people worship God in spite of adverse circumstances and the weight of having to live or cope with it. Often, loyal people demonstrate a sticking power with who they follow, regardless of how bad the situation may look at that time. Faith is often developed when it is tested through adversities and by the adversary. People often perceive the testing of their faith as a personal, spiritual attack and not as part of the process of developing their faith. It is when people see faith development moments as a personal attack that it becomes very challenging for them to see God in the midst of an attack. "My brethren, count it all joy when you fall into various temptations, knowing that the testing of your faith produces patience. But let patience have *its* perfect work, that you may be perfect and complete, lacking nothing" (James 1:2–4). Faith is the substance that creates the intimate moments with God.

The day before my 63rd birthday, I was out running various errands in preparation to celebrate my special day with family. I chose to wear a one-of-a-kind, handmade necklace designed with rubies, sapphires, and other precious stones. It was like wearing a rainbow around my neck with a large ruby in the center. Later that evening, as I felt for my necklace to remove it from my neck, I couldn't locate it. With great disappointment, I found it wasn't anywhere near me. I looked high and low for it. I told my family members what had happened and asked them to keep an eye out for my necklace. The next day, on the morning of my birthday, I woke up and was reminded that the necklace I hoped to wear was lost. However, God used this as an opportunity for me to see Him as the substance of things hoped for and the evidence of things not seen.

This revelation as it related to my necklace opened and illumined my understanding that God is the substance of everything I hope for and things I can't see yet with my natural eyes. I began to worship God and saw Him as the One who created the precious stones and the designer who constructed the necklace. I saw Him as the One who had provided the resources I needed to buy the necklace. My mindset, or my thought process, went from worrying about a necklace I lost and the feeling of powerlessness to looking to God through worship, to a God who had all power in His hands. This new mindset created an intimate moment with God by faith. This experience helped me see that Jesus chooses to respond in challenging situations by faith rather than react in challenging situation with no faith. The best response is to worship while facing adversities or the adversary. Worship is to acknowledge God as the One who created the winds and the waves, which are both subject to obey Him. Here are the questions God asks us: Do you believe who I am in the midst of your adversities? Do you believe that the things you don't have are your justification not to invest in faith? Do you have the faith to overcome, knowing that all things are possible for those who believe?

"Jesus said to him, 'If you can believe, all things *are* possible to him who believes'" (Mark 9:23). God is powerful. He is omniscient and faithful in who He is. True worshippers see God for who He is in every step they take, regardless of adversities or uncertainties they face. "For the eyes of the LORD run to and fro throughout the whole earth, to show Himself strong on behalf of *those* whose heart *is* loyal to Him" (2 Chron. 16:9).

"My brethren, count it all joy when you fall into various trials, knowing that the testing of your faith produces patience. But let patience have *its* perfect work, that you may be perfect and complete, lacking nothing" (James 1:2-4). Patience is developed with the understanding that trials, adversities, and the adversary are often used by God as tools to show people that He is God and that He is God all by Himself. Our trust in God is built from having intimate moments with Him designed by faith. "And we know that all things work together for good to those who love God, to those who are the called according to *His* purpose" (Rom. 8:28). The good news is that Jesus is the substance of what faith is.

I found my necklace on my birthday. I had to backtrack my steps. I recalled shopping at Macy's in a nearby mall. I called the store's customer service department the next morning and asked if anyone had found a necklace and turned it in to their lost and found. They asked me to describe the necklace. After I described it, they said they had locked it up and it was there for me to pick up. My necklace was intact, and I was happy to retrieve it. And I praised the Lord for what He had done and for who He is.

The Word empowers believers to trust God in spite of the challenges. Those who believe in the Word are a great cloud of witness of God's faithfulness. This same Word that lives vibrantly inside of them validates everything God said will come to pass. Believers have a great number of witnesses who can concur that God is faithful, especially during times of tests, trials, and adversities.

> *Therefore we also, since we are surrounded by so great a cloud of witnesses, let us lay aside every weight, and the sin which so easily ensnares us, and let us run with endurance the race that is set before us, looking unto Jesus, the author and finisher of our faith, who for the joy that was set before Him endured the cross, despising the shame, and has sat down at the right hand of the throne of God.*
> —Heb. 12:1-2

Jesus, who is the author and finisher of our faith, is the substance that faith is made of and the same substance required to build a personal relationship with God. Jesus is that substance of knowing God and the evidence of the things hoped for in knowing Him. In the process of knowing God through Jesus, our levels of anxiety will increase based on uncertainty and doubt; however, God, who is omniscient, shares with others not to be overwhelmed with anxiety but to purposely worship Him and give Him praise, and He will give a peace that is more powerful than what we consider normal in order to accept what is not normal—a new normal of living and thinking. "Be careful for nothing; but in every thing by prayer and supplication with thanksgiving let your requests be made known unto God. And the peace of God, which passeth all understanding, shall keep your hearts and minds through Christ Jesus" (Phil. 4:6–7 KJV).

John 15:14–15 says, "You are My friends if you do whatever I command you. No longer do I call you servants, for a servant does not know what his master is doing; but I have called you friends, for all things that I heard from My Father I have made known to you." God loved you so much that He believed you were worth dying for. God's love for believers is so big, so wide, and so deep that He sees us as His world. What is so amazing about God's love toward the mindset of the bride of Christ is that we rock his world! "For God so loved the world, that He gave His only begotten Son, that whoever believes in Him should not perish but have everlasting life" (John 3:16). God loves you so much that He sent His only Son to establish a personal relationship with you. Jesus became God's Word in the flesh so that in the Spirit we can have life with God eternally. When God sent Jesus, He not only sent His Word but He also gave His Word as a guarantee for believers to have life and to have it abundantly. God has a passionate, unique, vital, loving, and intimate personal relationship with those who are chosen and believe they are God's world.

"And I say also unto thee, that thou art Peter, and upon this rock I will build my church; and the gates of hell shall not prevail against it. And I will give unto thee the keys of the kingdom of heaven: and whatsoever thou shalt bind on earth shall be bound in heaven: and whatsoever thou shalt loose on earth shall be loosed in heaven" (Matt. 16:18–19 KJV). Having intimate moments with Jesus in the midst of impossibilities is like walking on water and having the faith to help maintain the walk

FAITH IS A DIFFERENT PAIR OF LENSES

in every ordered step. "For we walk by faith, not by sight (2 Cor. 5:7 KJV). As followers of Jesus, we spend a lot of energy practicing how to become like Jesus rather than simply believing we are like Him already. To believe we are like Him comes through having a personal, intimate relationship and not practicing religion. As followers of Jesus Christ, we are much more like Him than we think and believe. We were created and design to carry His Spirit in us. For people to see who God is and how seeing Him relates to their purpose, faith must become their new way of perception. "For in Him we live and move and have our being, as also some of your own poets have said, 'For we are also His offspring'" (Acts 17:28). Intimacy fosters a new way of embracing faith as it works in a never-been-done-before place. Intimacy with Jesus is found in our faith. Your faith illuminates your intimacy with Jesus.

This is the day that the Lord has made. And God empowers His followers to rejoice and be glad in it. Letting the same mind of Jesus be in you is like wearing a pair of corrective lenses that empowers the thought process of individuals to have the keys to the kingdom of heaven. God is so faithful that Jesus as His only begotten Son was persecuted and crucified. God said in Matthew 3:17. "This is My beloved Son, in whom I am well pleased." God shares in Hebrews 11:6 (KJV), "But without faith it is impossible to please him: for he that cometh to God must believe that he is, and that he is a rewarder of them that diligently seek him." God is so faithful that He submits himself to His Word. Moreover, that faith is so powerful that it gets God's full, undivided attention every time people worship Him. "Greater love has no one than this, than to lay down one's life for his friends" (John 15:13). God is so awesome in His strategic planning for people that He will purposely place them in adversity along with surrounding challenges. It's one thing to say because He lives I can face tomorrow; it's another thing to be a game-changer when you believe Philippians 4:13 (KJV), which tells us, "I can do all things through Christ which strengtheneth me."

Fear-not moments for believers are opportunities for faith to show up. Faith to believers is their new way of perception versus the old way of seeing or thinking. This new mindset becomes the new way for them to live, move, and function effectively in their purpose. This new mindset stops religion from getting in the way of having a personal relationship with God through Jesus who is the way. People often feel they are waiting on God, but rather it is God who is waiting on them to get to know the God who lives and moves to serve a purpose in them. Faith guides individuals to learn to pray with God rather than pray to God. Talking with God stems from having a personal relationship with God and not with religion, which teaches people to pray to Him. God purposes Jesus to rest in the midst of a storm so people can find rest in believing and following who He is when they are faced with adversity or the adversary. "Take my yoke upon you, and learn of me; for I am meek and lowly in heart: and ye shall find rest unto your souls. For my yoke is easy, and my burden is light" (Matt. 11:29–30 KJV).

To have a thought process that knows Jesus by way of an intimate relationship is different than grasping on to religious routines that give a misconception of where He is. God illustrates to us that greater is He who is in us than he who is in the world. Faith requires us to be transformed with the renewal of how we think by taking on the same mindset that is in Jesus. The transformation process allows individuals to believe that the same Jesus who walked on water is the same One who lives, moves, and functions in them by His Spirit. Having the mindset of Jesus empowers individuals to walk by faith and not according to their current thought process. Too often followers become emotionally tired and doubtful just before reaching their destiny or their appointed time. It is in these moments that faith needs to work harder, although difficulties will come and share the same space with faith. At times it is hard to imagine how some people can be so close to reaching their destination and purpose while learning to balance faith and the unexpected challenges just prior to their appointed time. The Centers for Disease Control and Prevention (CDC) reports that more than 3,500 people die from drowning each year in the United States. Drowning is the fifth most common accidental death in the United States. Healthline writes, "Drowning is a form of death by suffocation. Death occurs after the lungs take in water.... Every year, people drown in bathtubs, shallow

FAITH IS A DIFFERENT PAIR OF LENSES

lakes, and even small puddles.... Some studies indicate that a person can drown in 1 milliliter of fluid for every kilogram they weigh. So, a person weighing around 140 pounds (63.5 kg) could drown after inhaling only a quarter cup of water."[1] According to the National Highway Traffic Safety Administration (NHTSA), about 52 percent of accidents happen in a five-mile radius of a person's home, and about 69 percent of all car accidents happen ten miles from home."[2] Within the first two years after my two youngest children got their driver's licenses, they had four car accidents between the two of them. Two happened less than 12 feet from our home as they pulled out of the driveway and hit a neighbor's parked car. The other two accidents took place less than four miles from our house. I find it very interesting that some can be very close to home, and for whatever reason, something—an unexpected adversity—easily distracts them from reaching their appointed time or destination.

Just prior to reaching the appointed time, faith becomes more essential and vital than at any other point during the journey to destiny. It is when people are closer to reaching their purpose that faith operates best in the situation, circumstance, or substance. Hope becomes the only evidence you have to bring you through the adversity and reach the appointed time. It is toward the end of journey that faith helps you see God bigger than any adversity standing in the way of your purpose. The closer you are in reaching your appointed time, the more difficult the challenges. These challenges are used by God to bring you closer to Him by believing you can do all things in Jesus who strengthens you.

"We are of God, little children, and have overcome them: because greater is he that is in you, than he that is in the world" (1 John 4:4 KJV). "My sheep hear my voice, and I know them, and they follow me" (John 10:27 KJV). Jesus's voice moves the Holy Spirit to speak to our sprit, which empowers followers to hear Jesus's voice. The Holy Spirit is like a conduit who works as an intercessor between the called and Jesus, who

---

1. Kathryn Watson, "Drowning Facts and Safety Precautions," *Healthline*, https://www.healthline.com/health/how-long-does-it-take-to-drown
2. "Many Car Accidents Occur Close to Home," *Pines Salomon*, https://seriousaccidents.com/blog/many-car-accidents-occur-close-to-home/

made the call. This role of the Holy Spirit is between them who are called and Jesus, the One who called them. Because faith is a tool to help create intimacy with God through Jesus, all distractions from a mindset that doesn't seek Jesus's mindset are laid aside.

> *Therefore we also, since we are surrounded by so great a cloud of witnesses, let us lay aside every weight, and the sin which so easily ensnares us, and let us run with endurance the race that is set before us, looking unto Jesus, the author and finisher of our faith, who for the joy that was set before Him endured the cross, despising the shame, and has sat down at the right hand of the throne of God.*
> —Heb. 12:1–2

"This *is* the day the LORD has made; we will rejoice and be glad in it" (Ps. 118:24). When God made the day, it's the same format He used to form the world and everything in it by His Word. God is sharing with readers and listeners that it is by faith and by the substance of things hoped for and the evidence of things not seen that we get to God at His core. Too often, with the adversities of any day, people do not believe God who instructs them to walk by faith and not by sight. God says that without faith, it is impossible to please Him. The word *please* can be exchanged for the words *ask*, *request*, or *beg*. For believers to move from "this is the day the Lord has made" to "we will rejoice and be glad in it" requires a leap of faith, especially when they are faced with uncertainty. This leap of faith positions people to trust God through worship before seeing with their natural eyes how they think the day will turn out. The process enables people to trust the plan of God and that everything will work out for their good and for His glory. It takes faith to trust God. Faith is rooted in the personal relationship we have with Jesus and in believing that the same powerful, living Word lives inside of you. God so loved people that He gave the best thing He had, hoping it would be the very evidence that would produce an intimate, personal relationship with Him through His Son.

FAITH IS A DIFFERENT PAIR OF LENSES

Worship preceded by faith will awaken your promise every time. Seeds of greatness often lie dormant before reaching their purpose and at times may seem like they're not there at all. As followers, our promises may appear to be asleep, but they are not dead. They are just waiting to be transformed through faith and awakened to show our destiny. Getting to the real you and understanding your true identity is a process that begins with seeking the kingdom of God. This process is a journey that starts with a seed. This seed will keep you focused on what to look for as you approach the core of who God is. You can liken the process to getting to the core of an apple; the outside layer is peeled away, and the flesh of the apple is eaten before the seeds are revealed. You have to peel away your preconceptions of who God is before you are able to taste and see that the Lord is good. Ultimately, you will reach the seed of who God is inside of you. Followers will come to an understanding through the revelation of their purpose.

Seeking the kingdom of God is a life's journey that starts with a seed. The purpose of the seed is so much bigger than it appears to the naked eye, and it requires faith. Have hope through God's revelation in Jesus that this seed will develop into an apple. Jeremiah 1:5 (KJV) teaches us, "Before I formed thee in the belly I knew thee; and before thou camest forth out of the womb I sanctified thee, and I ordained thee a prophet unto the nations." One of the many glories of God is that He sees His people as complete. Before your mother gave birth to you, God had already created you and decreed who you would be. God is faithful to His Word and is slow to anger because He sees the end result from the beginning. The steps of a righteous person are ordered, and God remains in control. In the chaos, you will discover the seeds of greatness.

Chapter 7

MARY, WHY ARE YOU WEEPING?

Tests, trials, tribulations, and adversities often prepare followers for the promise while they are going through the process. As followers, we become closer to God while we are going through the process. Tests that may appear to be adversities sent by God are used to help His followers see Jesus in the midst of the adversity. God may choose to use these adversities to help change the way we think about God. Often when people are faced with adversity, they choose to react rather than respond to it. The test is to change our perception of setbacks, disappointments, and hardships and see them through faith (the eyes of God). These circumstances that appear to be setbacks may bring us closer to our destiny. Knowing how to think correctly will effectively work out the challenges we often feel when we're going through a difficult period. The reward of having our faith tested is not the passing of the test but knowing what we are made of in Jesus, who is the substance of our faith.

In John 20:15, Jesus considers Mary Magdalene's thought process before telling her what she needed to hear in order to be made whole. He asked her, "Why are you weeping?" and "Whom are you seeking?" The physical church of today has become a place similar to the tomb where

A CHANGED MINDSET

Jesus was once laid. Of course, Jesus is no longer in the tomb. However, He continually asks us, "Why are you weeping?" Too many followers of Jesus are crying because they are looking for Jesus in a building, an organization, a system, or a religion. However, He keeps knocking and waiting to move from a place where we first heard of Him to a place where He wants to live within us. It is in Jesus that we live, move, and have our purpose. The Holy Spirit works as a facilitator, along with Jesus, by revealing our purpose and identifying the role we play in God's plan. As followers, we attend church to give ourselves back to God through worship, to see God in every gift He has given us, and to see Him in the joy of our giving. The church service should promote followers to seek the kingdom of God in their daily activities, especially after the service has ended. As followers of Christ, our worship should be shown in how we live our daily lives around others rather than having Sunday church services as our only time of worship.

"Jesus said to her, 'Mary!' She turned and said to Him, 'Rabboni!' (which is to say, Teacher). Jesus said to her, 'Do not hold on to Me, for I have not yet ascended to My Father; but go to My brethren and say to them, "I am ascending to My Father and your Father, to My God and your God"'" (John 20:16–17). God tests our faith as part of our spiritual homework to show us where He is as we seek Him. Mary's faith was tested in her understanding of who Jesus is when she was faced with adversity. The testing of our faith strengthens our spiritual development by increasing the patience we need for the process. The church is the bride of Christ, created with the purpose of being perfectly aligned with Jesus as the bridegroom. So why do we allow ourselves to get so bent out of shape when we are faced with a test? All of us have faced loss, hardship, and pain as part of our lives. There is nothing wrong with crying. It can be a good thing, but we need to remember that God has us in the palm of His hand and has control of the outcome.

The difference between the mindset of a 21st century virgin and the mindset of the bride of Christ is the perception of who Jesus is in everyday circumstances. "You intended to harm me, but God intended it for good to accomplish what is now being done, the saving of many lives" (Gen. 50:20 NIV). God doesn't find pleasure in seeing His children suffer in the midst of adversity. There are occasions when God tests our faith or love, which causes us to wonder whether these tests are intended to destroy us or give us life. The answer, of course, depends on how we think. The testing of our faith is not meant to destroy the individual but rather to destroy a poor perception of Jesus and replace it with a stronger version. The mindset of a 21st century virgin sees the road to purpose filled with challenges and impossible adversities. The mindset of the bride of Christ knows that all things are possible when living life with purpose through Jesus. Being aligned with Jesus as His bride has its benefits; one of them is knowing who we are in His eyes.

God is present in our lives to effectively respond to our trials, tribulations, and life's lessons with love, grace, and mercy. God's grace doesn't always remove mountains or obstacles in our path, but it does give us the strength and a strategy to overcome them. God is always present, even when we throw pity parties, although He doesn't accept invitations to such events. Instead, God waits for us to see Him and understand the role He plays in our situation. Philippians 4:4 (NIV) says, "Rejoice in the Lord always. I will say it again: Rejoice!" If you feel you need to cry, then cry, because you know the victory will soon come. Cry out with praise as you glorify God. Cry out with thanksgiving that God loves you so much and intended you to be a blessing.

> *Let your gentleness be known to all men. The Lord is hand. Be anxious for nothing, but in everything by prayer and supplication, with thanksgiving, let your requests be made known to God; and the peace of God, which surpasses all understanding, will guard your hearts and minds through Christ Jesus. Finally, brethren, whatever things are true, whatever things* are *noble, whatever things* are *just, whatever things* are *pure, whatever things* are *lovely, whatever things* are *of good report, if* there is *any virtue and if* there is *anything praiseworthy—meditate on these things.*
> —Phil. 4:5–8

God uses ordinary people and everyday circumstances to encourage others not to quit when they're experiencing feelings of discouragement and disappointment in the transformation process. Often in this process, the gap between your anointing and the appointed time can be puzzling. It is also challenging and at times painful before change takes place. The other night I had a dream that my breast was engorged with milk. It was painful, enlarged, and heavy. In my dream I was given a baby to nurse, and in doing so, I felt so much better. I felt relief from the pressure and the discomfort from my breast. I understood from the dream that gifts, anointings, callings, and blessings that God gives can come wrapped in painful challenges. Between the steps of the anointing time and the appointed time, you will have to cope with the painful, challenging lessons you learn from one step to the next. God will provide and make provisions for the gifts, blessings, callings, and anointings as He gives according to His purpose.

"Saith the Lord of hosts, if I will not open you the windows of heaven, and pour you out a blessing, that there shall not be room enough to receive it" (Mal. 3:10 KJV). In my dream where I was at the point of feeling uncomfortable, God foresaw how it was going to turn out for my good and for His glory. God used my overflow of milk as my anointing and connected it with a baby who was hungry as my appointed time. The overflow of my breast was my anointing, and my appointing time was to feed and nourish a hungry baby. I was created to serve a baby who gave my purpose meaning. That is where the anointing meets the appointed time, wrapped both with pain and pleasure. God gives people a purpose to serve the needs of others. Our purpose is to give our gift, knowing that the fruit it bears belongs to others as beneficiaries and as God intended. God is our only living example of how purpose works and how to live on purpose. It is both pain and pleasure that pair together to give birth to purpose. So Mary, why are you weeping? This question is not meant to underline Mary's feelings for her personal loss of the Lord she loves. It is to challenge her thought process that pain and pleasure, blessings and bitterness, faith and fear work for the good of all things to those who are called. Learning to understand normal, bipolar emotions becomes the wonder twins necessary to walk by faith in the mindset of the bride of Christ. "I know how to be abased, and I know how to abound. Everywhere and in all things I have learned both to be full and to be hungry, both to abound and to suffer need. I can do all things through Christ who strengthens me" (Phil. 4:12–13).

When I was a child, I accepted Jesus as my Lord, although I didn't learn until much later that it was God who chose me. However, I remember sharing with my younger brother and uncle that I was saving myself for the Lord's use. They responded with laughter as they quickly began to make fun of me. Being a member of God's boot camp is not easy, so expect to be picked on and kicked around by others. This type of activity is often used to build spiritual character within us. Spiritual boot camp prepares you to be a warrior for Christ by transforming your thinking process from a 21st century virgin mindset to the mindset of a bride of Christ. What makes it so hard and painful is that the process often causes people to become separated from others and broken into pieces from who they thought they were. God will rearrange the broken pieces of their old mindset and change it into a mindset that thinks like the bride of Christ.

The amount of time for individuals to complete spiritual boot camp lies in accepting and embracing the process. Lessons in our spiritual homework assignments from God do not disappear; if they are disregarded, they return again and again. The same lessons are repeated, although with a different teacher. The process of spiritual boot camp is bitter and sweet. The bitterness of boot camp is the struggle associated with working out our faith. The struggle associated in the process forces followers to learn to love the challenge of seeking the God who lives inside of them. Only after we go through the process are we ready for the Master's use and able to experience the sweet taste of victory and the intimate relationship obtained with Jesus.

John 9:1–41 tells us of a young, blind man who Jesus healed, giving back his sight. The people of his town were amazed since the young man had been blind his entire life. Some thought he was born that way because of his parents. They were more interested in the reasons behind why he became blind than in the moment he received his sight. Jesus told the crowd that the young man was not blind because of the sins of his parents but rather so God may be glorified. I often found myself quick to condemn others and myself for things that appeared to be failures. Looking for blame in others as a quick solution gives us a limited perception and understanding of the whole story. But God in His awesome wisdom, grace, and mercy can change our perceptions as He reveals Himself in our thought process. As children of God, we have in our lives both success and failure. It is so easy to feel sorry for ourselves and indulge in self-pity. But the Lord's creative hand can mold and reshape our mistakes into something much bigger than the way we think of ourselves or the narrative we once wrote. So why are you crying, complaining, or questioning God about the spiritual homework assigned to help you succeed?

The first step in the transformation process from the mindset of a 21st century virgin to the mindset of a bride of Christ is to see challenges for what they are and know that God has an expected end for everything He starts. "For I know the thoughts that I think toward you, says the LORD, thoughts of peace and not of evil, to give you a future and a hope" (Jer. 29:11). Your challenges do not affect the anointing God has placed on your life, nor do your circumstances or situations. At times, the steps in the process may be painful and uncomfortable, but they will not be unbearable. It is not necessarily the lesson that is most important, but rather what we have learned on the way to understanding that lesson. Needless to say, if we as followers seek the kingdom of heaven first, the process will be much shorter in discovering who we are in God's eyes and how it relates to our purpose in life. Our purpose has already been established before our life ever began. "Before I formed you in the womb I knew you, before you were born I sanctified you; I ordained you a prophet to the nations" (Jer. 1:5). Jesus knows us because we were a spirit pregnant with destiny before our parents conceived us.

> *Then the scribes and Pharisees brought to Him a woman caught in adultery. And when they had set her in the midst, they said to Him, "Teacher, this woman was caught in adultery, in the very act. Now Moses, in the*

> law, commanded us that such should be stoned. But what do You say?" This they said, testing Him, that they might have something of which to accuse Him. But Jesus stooped down and wrote on the ground with His finger, as though He did not hear. So when they continued asking Him, he raised Himself up and said to them, "He who is without sin among you, let him throw a stone at her first." And again He stooped down and wrote on the ground. Then those who heard it, being convicted by their conscience, went out one by one, beginning with the oldest even to the last. And Jesus was left alone, and the woman standing in the midst. When Jesus had raised Himself up and saw no one but woman, He said to her, "Woman, where are those accusers of yours? Has no one condemned you?" She said, "No one, Lord." And Jesus said to her, "Neither do I condemn you; go and sin no more."
>
> —John 8:3–11

In this instance, Jesus made an example of a woman who was being accused, threatened, ostracized, and condemned to death by stoning by the religious leaders. What is so amazing about this story is how Jesus clearly illustrated that He had the authority to be judge over both life and death, the One who can forgive sin. Because Jesus is omniscient, He already knew He would be the sacrificial Lamb to die in our place and for our sins. As a result, we are no longer looked upon by God as sinners but as the bride of Christ. The challenge is that we as followers who have not had our minds and hearts fully transformed and changed will still see ourselves as sinners and not as new creatures in Christ Jesus. Jesus asked the woman, "Where are your accusers?" after they all had left. Perhaps we should ask ourselves the same question and know that through Christ, no one can defeat us because His Word has made us whole, and we are changed.

The woman who was accused by others also had to deal with the stuff she accused herself of. Jesus just didn't remove her accusers; He also made her whole by removing what she thought of herself.

A CHANGED MINDSET

> *As you therefore have received Christ Jesus the Lord, so walk in Him, rooted and built up in Him and established in the faith, as you have been taught, abounding in it with thanksgiving. Beware lest anyone cheat you through philosophy and empty deceit, according to the tradition of men, according to the basic principles of the world, and not according to Christ. For in Him dwells all the fullness of the Godhead bodily; and you are complete in Him, who is the head of all principality and power.*
> —Col. 2:6–10

Jesus caused the woman's accusers to leave without causing her any harm. He pointed out her low self-esteem and showed her accusers that the One who is life is much greater than anyone who was judging the woman. The mindset of a 21st century virgin can be seen in how the woman accused of adultery viewed herself. "The eyes of your understanding being enlightened; that you may know what is the hope of His calling, what are the riches of the glory of His inheritance in the saints" (Eph. 1:18). What if the greatest mistake any follower could make in life was to fail to see his or her true God-given purpose? I wonder how many followers are, like Mary, weeping for the wrong reasons.

Chapter 8

GOD IS PREDETERMINED

God is predetermined to transform the mindset of the 21st century virgin into a mindset that thinks like the bride of Christ. The process of transforming the mindset of the 21st century virgin is what sets us free. In this transformation, the mind changes from an old way of thinking to a new thought process. The end result of this process puts Christ in how we think and gives us the ability to see and understand who we are in the eyes of God. "Therefore if the Son makes you free, you shall be free indeed" (John 8:36).

This changed mindset gives birth to a new creature in Christ Jesus. It gives rise to a change in our thinking and a direct influence on our behavior. His patience is endless, and His love is deep despite the numerous failed initial attempts by the 21st century virgin mindset to understand the importance of having a personal relationship with God.

The Virgin Mary was chosen to be Jesus's natural mother. She was tremendously favored, anointed, and appointed by God as a conduit to bring the Son of God into the world. Similar to the mindset of the 21st century virgin, she came into her purpose first as a virgin and later as a bride. In her own time, Mary was in danger of being rejected by her family, her culture, and her fiancé, Joseph, who believed she broke her promise to him since she appeared no longer to be a virgin. Furthermore, the law threatened to kill her because she was pregnant before marriage. How awesome that God in His great majesty would choose a woman who was viewed by society as impure to be the mother of His Son. God saw Mary pregnant with purpose and saw the mindset of the 21st century virgin pregnant with promise before taking on the mindset of the bride of Christ.

"Jesus said to her, 'Woman, why are you weeping? Whom are you seeking?' She, supposing Him to be the gardener, said to Him, 'Sir, if you have carried Him away, tell me where You have laid him, and I will take Him away'" (John 20:15). Mary is feeling distressed, hopeless, and alone because she believed Jesus was dead. She had every reason to weep because she had suffered a huge loss, yet this man asks why she is weeping. Christ's first question articulated thoughtfulness and concern for Mary; his second question shows us that He knows the cause of her grief and is capable of helping her find the man she is searching for. Jesus gives Mary's mindset a 180-degree turn so she can see that she is looking at the same Lord she seeks, and He is risen. Her thinking process was transformed from mourning the loss of someone she loved to a changed mindset of celebrating the resurrected victory of knowing who Jesus is.

When we take on this renewed mindset, Jesus is revealed to us for who He is at His core. The outcome from having this mindset in Christ is a blessed assurance that His peace is perfect in times of trouble or weeping. It is this mindset that unlocks dark places that keep us bound by depression and emotional pain. The mindset of the bride of Christ embraces struggles rather than being a victim or reacting to pain. Like a savvy chess player, this new mindset looks at potential challenges to come from the opponent's point of view and then moves strategically to be the head and not the tail. The mindset of the bride of Christ embraces difficult challenges by looking to see where Jesus is in the midst of everything. "I will instruct you and teach you in the way you should go; I will guide you with My eye" (Ps. 32:8).

There are times when adversity will foster a trusting relationship with Jesus, even during the storm as opposed to when the storm is over. The 21st century virgin mindset asks God, "Where are you?" The bride of Christ mindset will say to Him, "God, even when I can't trace your face, I know You are omnipresent." "They should seek the Lord, in the hope that they might grope for Him and find Him, though He is not far from each one of us" (Acts 17:27).

I had a dream that I was sitting in the passenger seat of a convertible car with Jesus in the driver's seat. The car stopped as we watched an object falling from the sky. I was amazed and initially thought it might be debris from a nearby tornado. As I continued to stare at the falling object, it appeared to me that it was a house falling from the sky, headed in our direction. I pleaded with Jesus to move the car so the house wouldn't fall on top of us, but He didn't move. When the object finally came to earth where I could see it for what it was, I saw that it was only a dresser, not a house. I understood the lesson God was teaching me that no weapons formed against me will prosper.

When we are in alignment with God, we share His same mindset. What appears to be a house coming down on us may turn out to be something far smaller that will not kill us, although it may be frightening. It is only to remind us that greater is He who is in us than he who is in the world. "Surely he shall deliver thee from the snare of the fowler, and from the noisome pestilence. He shall cover thee with his feathers, and under his wings shalt thou trust: his truth shall be thy shield and buckler. Thou shalt not be afraid for the terror by night; nor for the arrow that flieth by day; nor for the pestilence that walketh in darkness; nor for the destruction that wasteth at noonday" (Ps. 91:3-6). God wants us to look at challenges in life as a test of our faith in Him and as an opportunity for Him to reveal Himself to us as our heavenly Father and protector. We worship him because of who He is at His core—awesome, strong, powerful, faithful to His Word, and mighty, just to name a few. Worship is the ability to praise God using descriptions of who He is at His core. Regardless of what we are facing and where we are in the process of transformation and change, He is our protector and our provider, and He is faithful to those who are called according to His purpose.

God always has you in His thoughts and in His hands when you are living through a season of struggle. "But as for you, you meant evil

A CHANGED MINDSET

against me; *but* God meant it for good, in order to bring it about as *it is* this day, to save many people alive" (Gen. 50:20). God never finds pleasure in seeing people suffer as a result of adversities. Times of trial are designed to ultimately bring about a change, much like the pain of labor leads to childbirth. God is set on transforming the 21st century virgin mindset into the mindset of the bride of Christ. When God looks into the mindset of the 21st century virgin, He sees His church that He loves and for whom He is waiting patiently to become aligned with Him so its purpose might be fulfilled. The chastisements along the way in the process could be likened to a ghastly storm of hopelessness. But in all cases, God, through His infinite wisdom and love, gives us His grace and mercy. His love may not remove the mountain or storm in our path, but He will teach us the way over the mountain or through the storm that we may gain His strength and trust while we're going through it. "But to each one of us grace was given according to the measure of Christ's gift" (Eph. 4:7).

The perfect peace of God gives us the ability to overcome any challenge through grace. A measure of grace is given to us at the moment of salvation, which is available at any point. However, we need to know how to access it. The answer doesn't lie in feeling sorry for ourselves or crying out of bitterness to God. The mindset of the bride of Christ knows that the grace and peace of God come from a personal relationship with Jesus and knowing that His joy dwells in us. "Rejoice in the Lord always. Again I will say, rejoice!" (Phil. 4:4). The mindset of the bride of Christ cries out in joy knowing that in Christ there is victory and that He operates from within. It is this type of mindset in Christ Jesus that empowers followers to make a conscious decision to rejoice in the Lord and be glad while working through the process and not losing hope or sight of their destiny. Sometimes what appears to be failure is actually an event God has orchestrated for our own good and for His glory. The Lord is constantly molding and reshaping us for His glory. The challenge lies in having the same mind as Christ Jesus so we are open to being used for something much bigger than ourselves and beyond our limited imaginations. "My son, do not despise the chastening of the LORD, nor

GOD IS PREDETERMINED

detest His correction; for whom the LORD loves He corrects, just as a father the son *in whom* he delights" (Prov. 3:11-12).

Over the past few years, I have put in so much hard work toward my educational goals. Through all the ups and downs, I realized I must learn to trust God in every circumstance. "Trust in the LORD with all your heart, and lean not on your own understanding" (Prov. 3:5). There were times when I did not understand how God could love me and still allow me to go through life's storms without rescuing me from them. I realize now that it is God who controls the tempests and that He kept me anchored, even while I was begging Him to get me out of it. If He rescued me every time I prayed for a way out, I would never know Him as faithful or be a witness that His grace is enough. It was His grace and mercy that kept me from self-destruction or being destroyed by the storm. There are times when the steps He has ordered are necessary to reach our next level toward destiny.

> *Therefore, having been justified by faith, we have peace with God through our Lord Jesus Christ, through whom also we have access by faith into this grace in which we stand, and rejoice in hope of the glory of God. And not only that, but we also glory in tribulations, knowing that tribulation produces perseverance; and perseverance, character; and character, hope. Now hope does not disappoint, because the love of God has been poured out in our hearts by the Holy Spirit who was given to us.*
> —Rom. 5:1-6

The God we serve is not someone who just fixes things but is the master of design of all creativity. He wants to make us whole and not just treat our symptoms. In the mindset of the 21st century virgin, too often the body of Christ is waiting for God to make the next move while He is waiting for them to be transformed with a changed mindset that will follow Him. God's principles do not change, but the way He performs may vary depending on what we need. Because God is omniscient, He always knows how to perform, develop, and present ways that may seem unconformable for followers at first; however, He knows that all things do work out for their good. Therefore, we are called to not set our level of expectations for what God has planned for our destiny based on our past emotions, experiences, and history. In doing so, we may find ourselves being kept in a holding room where seemingly nothing is happening when, in fact, God is preparing something new that will turn our situations around.

> *Immediately Jesus made His disciples get into the boat and go before Him to the other side, while He sent the multitudes away. And when He had sent the multitudes away, He went up on the mountain by Himself to pray. Now when evening came, He was alone there. But the boat was now in the middle of the sea, tossed by the waves, for the wind was contrary. Now in the fourth watch of the night Jesus went to them, walking on the sea. And when the disciples saw Him walking on the sea, they were troubled, saying, "It is a ghost!" And they cried out for fear. But immediately Jesus spoke to them, saying, "Be of good cheer! It is I; do not be afraid." And Peter answered Him and said, "Lord, if it is You, command me to come to You on the water." So He said, "Come." And when Peter had come down out of the boat, he walked on the water to go to Jesus. But when he saw that the wind was boisterous, he was afraid; and beginning to sink he cried out, saying, "Lord, save me!" And immediately Jesus stretched out* His *hand and caught him, and said to him, "O you of little faith, why did you doubt?" And when they got into the boat, the wind ceased. Then those who were in the boat came and worshiped Him, saying, "Truly You are the Son of God."*
> —Matt. 14:22–33

As chosen vessels and followers of Jesus, we must eventually leave the boat, like Peter, or leave our people, like Abraham, and take a leap of faith by walking in our destiny. As it is written in Matthew 22:14, "For many are called, but few *are* chosen." The journey to our destiny is personal, and its steps have been customized for us as individuals. Because God is omniscient, He has already predetermined a way for us. It is through Jesus that we have access to God who holds our destiny. "If anyone comes to Me and does not hate his father and mother, wife and children, brothers and sisters, yes, and his own life also, he cannot be My disciple. And whoever does not bear his cross and come after Me cannot be My disciple" (Luke 14:26–27). The journey we take as followers of Jesus is one of faith, which He governs. We must come to realize that Jesus is the author and finisher of our faith, our steps, and how our story ends. Peter had enough faith to start walking toward Jesus on the water, but somewhere in the middle, he became distracted and forgot to put his faith fully in Jesus. Peter needed to know that to finish his journey, his faith had to rest in Jesus at all times. Jesus demonstrated that He was the finisher of Peter's faith, no matter what. Often the mindset of the 21st century virgin places too much attention on how the story starts or the things that happen in the middle of the story where Jesus, the author and finisher of our story, has predestined His bride to have a great end. "Being confident of this very thing, that He who has begun a good work in you will complete *it* until the day of Jesus Christ" (Phil. 1:6).

The secret to keeping your faith is keeping your spiritual eyes on Jesus and avoiding distraction. God so loved the world that He gave His only Son as a gift to us that we may have life as it already exists in heaven. "But God, who is rich in mercy, for his great love wherewith he loved us" (Eph. 2:4 KJV). God gave Jesus to the world to supplement their lack of faith in Him. The love God has for the world is intentional through Jesus to them who believe that the core of who He is will be governed by every adversity. Heaven comes to us in the form of Jesus. He demonstrated this by pulling Peter up when he could not finish the journey across the water alone. The steps of a righteous person are ordered to lead them into God's plan and purpose. These steps in the process teach us who God is and how we are knitted together to be closer to Jesus by faith. The ordered steps help us grow and trust in God's plan for us to succeed in our calling and purpose.

A CHANGED MINDSET

Seeking is part of the process followers go through to know who God is by living life with purpose. Too often we look for God to appear in the middle of a storm when in reality Jesus is already in the boat with us, but His thought process is so different that we question His peace of mind. During times of trial, the kingdom of God is revealed to us when we look *to* God instead of *for* God in the midst of trouble. According to the *Oxford Dictionary*, a *facilitator* is "a person or thing that makes an action or process easy or easier." Words that best describe a facilitator are organizer, architect, implementer, enabler, helper, originator, initiator, and catalyst. The Holy Spirit as a facilitator empowers the people of God by helping them build a relationship with the Father through the Son. The Holy Spirit is given as a power source that helps God's people successfully live out their destinies. He gives them the revelation needed for God's purpose for their lives. John 4:24 teaches us that "God is a Spirit: and they that worship him must worship him in spirit and in truth."

We are all holding an umbrella created by God that can protect us from any kind of weather; however, the strength of the umbrella is only equal to the level of our faith. Worship fosters faith and places us in the presence of God, granting us access to His core. Faith is the stuff that God uses to create from, and at the same time it is the same thing we use to hope for in that thing we ask. We cannot see it with our natural eye at this time, yet it is imaginable in our mind when our mind is stayed on Christ Jesus. Jesus, in whom we have our faith, empowers His followers to hope for things that have not yet been manifested. Jesus is the door, the lock, and the key to God's heart. The Holy Spirit reveals in us the truth of God concerning our purpose and desires. That same Spirit facilitates worship for God's followers in spirit and in truth, therefore revealing who God is.

> *But God has revealed them to us through His Spirit. For the Spirit searches all things, yes, the deep things of God. For what man knows the things of a man except the spirit of the man which is in him? Even so no one knows the things of God except the Spirit of God. Now we have received, not the*

> *spirit of the world, but the Spirit who is from God, that we might know the things that have been freely given to us by God. These things we also speak, not in words which man's wisdom teaches but which the Holy Spirit teaches, comparing spiritual things with spiritual. But the natural man does not receive the things of the Spirit of God, for they are foolishness to him; nor can he know them, because they are spiritually discerned. But he who is spiritual judges all things, yet he himself is rightly judged by no one. For "who has known the mind of the LORD that he may instruct Him?" But we have the mind of Christ.*
>
> —1 Cor. 2:10–16

The Holy Spirit as a facilitator guides the people of God into His truth.

> *Now Jesus and His disciples went out to the towns of Caesarea Philippi; and on the road He asked His disciples, saying to them, "Who do men say that I am?" So they answered, "John the Baptist; but some say, Elijah; and others, one of the prophets." He said to them, "But who do you say that I am?" Peter answered and said to Him, "You are the Christ." Then He strictly warned them that they should tell no one about Him.*
>
> —Mark 8:27–31

It was not flesh and blood that revealed this answer but rather the Holy Spirit. The call is for everyone who hears, and the Holy Spirit is acting under the authority of God to foster those who will answer the call. The Samaritan woman at the well had a calling to be an evangelist and was drawn to meet Jesus to learn how to fulfill her destiny. God may use an unexpected storm to draw us into the living water. God illustrates through our own abilities how it is the greater One who lives in us. The story of Jonah and the big fish is another example of how God used an external circumstance to bring out one of His followers'

A CHANGED MINDSET

powers beyond his own limitations. Many are called, but only one may rise to be chosen. Peter walked across water during the middle of the storm because the greater One who lived in him gave him the strength. The Holy Spirit, as the facilitator in our worship of God, helps us enter into His presence every day to show us our destiny. Worship empowers the people of God with faith to enter into His presence. When we seek God through worship and have the determination to uncover the kingdom of heaven, this righteousness fosters an awakening of the mindset of the 21st century virgin into a personal knowledge of God.

God allowed His people to become homeless after He expelled Adam and Eve from the Garden of Eden. When they left the garden, God had the opportunity to prepare for His bride a permanent home. Furthermore, it would be built on a relationship with Him through Jesus Christ where His bride would never be at risk of being homeless. The transformation from homelessness to living eternally with God requires various challenges and life's lessons that facilitate followers to seek Him at His core. God called out to Adam after the fall, asking where he was, although God knew exactly where Adam was both spiritually and naturally. In essence, God was stirring Adam's mind by asking him where he was in relationship to Him. Adam saw Eve as the one who gave life and called her the "mother of all living." But when a person looks to find their purpose in living creatures instead of in God the Creator, they will have to deal with the consequences. This decision will often lead to homelessness and not having an intimate, personal relationship with Jesus as His bride. There is hope for the mindset of the 21st century virgin to learn how to function as a citizen of the kingdom of heaven here on earth by way of transformation and a changed mindset.

"Let not your heart be troubled; you believe in God, believe also in Me. In My Father's house are many mansions; if *it were* not so, I would have told you. I go to prepare a place for you. And if I go and prepare a place for you, I will come again and receive you to Myself; that where I am, *there* you may be also. And where I go you know, and the way you know" (John 14:1–4). In the kingdom where Jesus has prepared a place for us, He has already planned our purpose and function as His brides. Jesus has prepared for us as citizens of the kingdom of heaven so much more than receiving three meals and a comfortable cot to sleep on. It is a role that has been designed for us as individuals as brides of Christ. The journey or process to the kingdom is based on our relationship with Jesus, who is the key and the way to knowing who we are and who God is. The 21st century virgin is born homeless and remains so until their mindset is changed to seek the kingdom of God. "For in pouring this fragrant oil on My body, she did *it* for My burial. Assuredly, I say to you, wherever this gospel is preached in the whole world, what this woman has done will also be told as a memorial to her" (Matt. 26:12-13). As Jesus prepared Himself for the crucifixion to His resurrection, He also facilitated followers through the Holy Spirit from seeing Him into being Him.

The Garden of Eden was never intended to be a permanent home for people, but rather our eternal home was built from the sacrificial blood of Jesus Christ.

> *For we know that if our earthly house, this tent, is destroyed, we have a building from God, a house not made with hands, eternal in the heavens. For in this we groan, earnestly desiring to be clothed with our habitation which is from heaven, if indeed, having been clothed, we shall not be found naked. For we who are in this tent groan, being burdened, not because we want to be unclothed, but further clothed, that mortality may be swallowed up by life. Now He who has prepared us for this very thing is God, who also has given us the Spirit as a guarantee. So we are always confident, knowing that while we are at home in the body we are absent from the Lord. For we walk by faith, not by sight. We are confident, yes, well pleased rather to be absent from the body and to be present with the Lord.*
>
> —2 Cor. 5:1–8

A CHANGED MINDSET

Jesus's resurrection was God's ultimate demonstration of His love for the homeless. The homeward journey at times is filled with more downs than ups, often packed with pain and uncertainty. Religion is not in itself the journey to the kingdom. The journey can be taken only through a personal, intimate relationship with Jesus. The church as an establishment for religious activities is not the way, but its purpose is to point to the way of the kingdom. As followers, we must do the homework by establishing our own personal, intimate relationship with God through Jesus. The search for the kingdom of God fosters knowing God and uncovers the mirror that reveals to us who we are as His bride by transforming the mindset of the 21st century virgin. Trusting in God leads us to a form of worship in which we exhale the truth of who God is. It is in this undertaking that we expose Him at His core.

People often misunderstand the mystery behind the kingdom of heaven. It is not a place we can literally touch and see, but it is a state of mind that is in the same mindset of Jesus. I explain to my son Tyrone that the kingdom of God is within us and around us. Nevertheless, because God is omnipresent, the kingdom of God is here on earth but lived in a different dimension by a changed mindset. God's intention is for followers to have access to the kingdom of God while searching for or living out your purpose on earth. The mindset of the bride of Christ Jesus is to learn how to balance both dimensions. The task can be very challenging since we must learn how to separate reality from illusions. Knowing the things that are important to God according to His Word and the grace He gives to overcome the things that are not important according to His Word can be considered illusions.

God so loved us that He gave His only begotten Son that we may have everlasting life through Him. Jesus is the key to the kingdom. It is only through His righteousness, not our own, that we begin the journey to enter into the Father's presence. When we are with Him, we stand on holy ground where our true purpose is revealed by His Spirit. In Jesus we live, move, and have our being. He is our only connection to productivity, our only link to our purpose.

GOD IS PREDETERMINED

I am the true vine, and My Father is the vinedresser. Every branch in Me that does not bear fruit He takes away; and every branch *that bears fruit He prunes, that it may bear more fruit. You are already clean because of the word which I have spoken to you. Abide in Me, and I in you. As the branch cannot bear fruit of itself, unless it abides in the vine, neither can you, unless you abide in Me. I am the vine, you* are *the branches. He who abides in Me, and I in him, bears much fruit; for without Me you can do nothing. If anyone does not abide in Me, he is cast out as a branch and is withered; and they gather them and throw* them *into the fire, and they are burned. If you abide in Me, and My words abide in you, you will ask what you desire, and it shall be done for you. By this My Father is glorified, that you bear much fruit; so you will be My disciples.*

—John 15:1–8

Sometimes waiting *for* God rather than waiting *in* God can put you at risk of becoming homeless. Waiting in God places the mindset of the bride of Christ in the position to worship Him in His presence and proclaim who He is. Waiting in God rather than waiting for Him will place you in a position to know that God's grace is more than enough to carry you through until your change comes. Deuteronomy 33:25 tells us, "Your sandals *shall be* iron and bronze; as your days, *so shall* your strength be." This type of waiting for God is proactive rather than passive, which encourages distraction, idleness, and doubt. The Israelites waited for Moses to return from the mountain with the Ten Commandments when they should have been waiting in God through worship and prayer. God's grace sufficiently covers His people and provides everything they need to confront any difficulty or challenge. Grace is undeserved favor; however, God is mindful of everything as relational to Him and His ways.

Chapter 9

GOD IS MINDFUL

The mindset of the 21st century virgin is on the mind of God. Hebrews 2:6–7 (KJV) tells us, "But one in a certain place testified, saying, 'What is man, that thou art mindful of him? or the son of man that thou visitest him? Thou madest him a little lower than the angels; thou crownedst him with glory and honour, and didst set him over the works of thy hands." Romans 3:23–24 says, "For all have sinned and fall short of the glory of God, being justified freely by His grace through the redemption that is in Christ Jesus." God loved the world so much that He gave His Word in the form of His only Son to show us how much He loves us.

Jesus became the first human example of God's love for mankind and the first true example of how we are to love God, ourselves, and others. He didn't stop there; God built His church on a strong and steady foundation that He built within us, a type of substance to withstand challenges. The Word of God keeps the mind of the 21st century virgin thought process from being distracted until the transformation is completed.

> *Because the foolishness of God is wiser than men; and the weakness of God is stronger than men. For ye see your calling, brethren, how that not many wise men after the*

A CHANGED MINDSET

flesh, not many mighty, not many noble, are called: but God hath chosen the foolish things of the world to confound the wise; and God hath chosen the weak things of the world to confound the things which are mighty; and base things of the world, and things which despised, hath God chosen, yea, and things which are not, to bring to naught things that are.
—1 Cor. 1:25–28 KJV

Jesus looks at the 21st century virgin mindset as a member of His body who may have had it rough and suffered greatly as a result of numerous poor life choices due to the lack of not having a closer relationship with Him. "And behold, a woman in the city who was a sinner, when she knew that *Jesus* sat at the table in the Pharisee's house, brought an alabaster flask of fragrant oil, and stood at His feet behind *Him* weeping; and she began to wash His feet with her tears, and wiped *them* with the hair of her head; and she kissed His feet and anointed *them* with the fragrant oil" (Luke 7:37–39). The 21st century virgin mindset becomes empowered to worship Jesus like the woman with the alabaster box. Your alabaster box of ointment can be what you have to offer—your voice, your hands, or any part of yourself you can use to worship God—but most of all the purpose God called you for.

The 21st century virgin mindset gives Jesus everything because Jesus has given everything, including His own life. The woman with the alabaster box demonstrated courage and boldness in her choice to worship Jesus through her gift of service. Everyone in the house questioned her actions, and the Pharisees as well as Simon deemed her behavior unacceptable. Jesus's response was that the woman had many sins but had asked for forgiveness and repented. He is looking for the same boldness from the mindset of the 21st century virgin in the transformation process to the mindset of the bride of Christ. He is looking for a committed love and an earnest desire to worship Him. The 21st century virgin mindset needs to find what God has placed inside of them, such as His love and His promises that what He started in them He will see to the finish. God is always in the process of moving the mindset of the 21st century virgin mindset toward a relationship with Him through Jesus.

In Luke 7:47–49, Jesus explains to Simon, "'Therefore I say to you, her sins, which *are* many, are forgiven, for she loved much. But to whom little is forgiven, *the same* loves little.' Then He said to her, 'Your sins are forgiven.' And those who sat at the table with Him began to say to themselves, 'Who is this who even forgives sins?'" During a church service, it's not hard to spot a 21st century virgin mindset sitting among the mindsets of the brides of Christ. The mindset of the bride of Christ seeks time to worship God at home, in their car, at work, or walking down the street in the same way God is looking for people taking moments to worship Him in their daily life's activities. The mindset of the bride of Christ is never ashamed of demonstrating gratitude and worship for who Christ is. On the other hand, the mindset of the 21st century virgin may shine due to feeling embarrassed from exhibiting this type of worship in public.

In 1 Corinthians 13:12, we read, "For now we see in a mirror, dimly, but then face to face. Now I know in part, but then I shall know just as I also am known.'" Paul speaks about dimly seeing the plan that God has for him, but I hope to be able to see the vision more clearly as Christ continues to increases within me. My conversation with God is no longer asking for what I want but rather asking for His will as my steps are ordered and governed toward spiritual growth and development. God plans for us to do good things and to live as He always intended for us to live. That is why He sent Christ to show us who we are in Him. God gives us the blueprints and the strategy through Jesus and the Holy Spirit to build the mindset of the bride of Christ Jesus. He has made available the resources needed to build it, but He is not going to put them directly into our hands with no appreciation. Rather, He makes them available as we learn to walk by faith. God has set in motion His plan and purpose for my life, even when I trip and fall flat on my face. He picks me up each time as a loving father would and prepares for me a feast in the presence of my enemies. What God has prepared for me is so much bigger than what I can ever perceive or obtain on my own. No

A CHANGED MINDSET

longer do I make Christ fit into my agenda, but rather I seek after how He has fitted me perfectly into His agenda.

Living is a process where survival is based only on instant gratification with no thought or hope for tomorrow. Pure survival is only a preparation for death. By choosing to really live, you are tapping into the tree of life and embracing the future plans God has for you and embracing Christ in your heart through faith. Stand firm, and be deeply rooted in His love. Your heart will always be where your treasure resides. Matthew 6:19–21 tells us, "Do not lay up for yourselves treasures on earth, where moth and rust destroy and where thieves break in and steal; but lay up for yourselves treasures in heaven, where neither moth nor rust destroys and where thieves do not break in and steal. For where your treasure is, there your heart will be also."

God loves you as His child and wants you to enjoy a relationship with Him. He is the answer to your search for that ultimate relationship. He will fill the holes in your heart and mend the broken pieces. He is the one Creator of the universe and all it contains, including you. You will not be complete inside until you have a personal relationship with God through Jesus. He is more than a concept; He is someone who knows you and who you are. He is someone who cares about you, your life, and your purpose for living. Faith is the substance in which the mind of the bride of Christ lives and moves and where purpose is revealed by His Spirit. Psalm 37:23 says, "The steps of a *good* man are ordered by the LORD, and He delights in his way." Isaiah 30:20 says, "And *though* the Lord gives you the bread of adversity and the water of affliction, yet your teachers will not be moved into a corner anymore, but your eyes shall see your teachers." When God orders your steps in the process of transformation, He does not always forewarn you. When He prepares the bread of adversity and the water of affliction, God as our Teacher has also prepared for you a way to overcome them. Do not allow them to distract you from God, your Teacher. They are merely tools to build your trust in Jesus. You are your trainer for discovering your purpose in life so you might have it more abundantly.

GOD IS MINDFUL

God promises that if you keep your mind on Jesus, He will give you perfect peace and will not forsake you. Do not allow the past or even your current situation to dictate your destiny or distract you from the steps God has placed before you. The question of "but what if?" is a trap the enemy puts on your path toward destiny. This particular mode of thinking takes place in the battlefield of the mind. We read in 2 Corinthians 10:4 (KJV), "For the weapons of our warfare are not carnal, but mighty through God to the pulling down of strong holds." Fear feeds the "but what if?" within, which subsequently encourages doubt and mistrust of God. The transformation process empowers you to think and then behave like Jesus. Throughout it all, it is important to remember how this process begins, which is with trust in Jesus even when you can't see Him. Learn how to build faith in times of seeing nothing on the horizon.

God uses the falls, the kicks, the rejection, and the isolation to mold and shape you into your purpose and make a new creation. Just as there is pain when a woman gives birth, so was there pain when Jesus shed His blood that we may be born into new life. The earth also suffers in labor, waiting to give birth to its God-given purpose. *For we know that the whole creation groans and labors with birth pangs together until now. Not only that, but we also who have the firstfruits of the Spirit, even we ourselves groan within ourselves, eagerly waiting for the adoption, the redemption of our body. For we were saved in this hope, but hope that is seen is not hope; for why does one still hope for what he sees? But if we hope for what we do not see, we eagerly wait for it with perseverance.—* Rom. 8:22–25 Being anointed comes with both blessings and challenges, but nothing is impossible for God and those who are called according to His purpose.

Chapter 10

THE MINDSET THAT FEEDS

"What would Jesus do?" is a question often asked from the mindset of the 21st century virgin. This perception is seeing Jesus as a God who lives on the outside as opposed to the One who lives and moves from within. The mindset of the bride of Christ understands that God dwells within us. Jesus teaches us to pray in Matthew 6:9-11 with the words, "Our Father in heaven, hallowed be Your name. Your kingdom come, Your will be done on earth, as *it is* in heaven. Give us this day our daily bread." The mindset of the bride of Christ knows Him intimately through praise and worship. This type of relationship with Jesus is a tool that is used as a weapon in spiritual warfare. The mindset of the bride of Christ doesn't wonder, "What would Jesus do?" because His bride knows He lives and moves from within as a result of their intimate, personal relationship.

Because the bride mindset is kept on Jesus Christ, there is a sense of perfect peace when faced with struggles. Isaiah 26:3 says, "You will keep *him* in perfect peace, *whose* mind *is* stayed *on You*, because he trusts in You." However, it is only when we go through storms that we as followers learn to put our trust in Jesus that we may walk toward our destiny. The mindset of the 21st century virgin has always been on the mind of God, even before the time she began the process of transforming into a new creature in the Potter's hand, being transformed and changed into a new creature.

A CHANGED MINDSET

Psalm 37:23 tells us, "The steps of a *good* man are ordered by the Lord, and He delights in his way." The steps God orders are designed to take us down the road of our destiny. Everything we learn along this road teaches us about the God who is within us. These steps are not always easily ordered or user-friendly. They may even cause us to trip, fall, or slow down. However, it's these ordered steps that promote our growth and development in becoming more like God at our core. Just as a potter takes a mound of clay to create a vessel, God molds us into new creations in Jesus Christ. The journey of becoming authentically who you are can be extremely challenging, but the Holy Spirit will empower those who seek first the kingdom of God.

During the process of discovering who you are in God, there is also a discovery of who God is in you. Seeking first the kingdom of God is truly the discovery of your own life, your function, and your destiny. Acts 13:22 (NIV) says, "I have found David son of Jesse, a man after my own heart; he will do everything I want him to do." David sought after God's heart because he found who he was in God. Needless to say, it all began when David started to search for who God is. To know God's heart is to know the issues that concern God and to have the desire to talk with Him about those issues, waiting for Him to move in you in His own time.

> *Therefore David inquired of the Lord, and He said, "You shall not go up; circle around behind them, and come upon them in front of the mulberry trees. And it shall be, when you hear the sound of marching in the tops of the mulberry trees, then you shall advance quickly. For then the Lord will go out before you to strike the camp of the Philistines." And David did so, as the Lord commanded him; and he drove back the Philistines from Geba as far as Gezer.*
> —2 Sam. 5:23–25

The process of knowing who God is within you may seem like a small step of faith, but it will produce much fruit in due time. This measure of faith is designed so followers may know that just a little bit of

THE MINDSET THAT FEEDS

God is enough to make a huge difference when seeking and discovering who He is in everyday circumstances. God purposely put His heart in David as a child so he would come to discover the God who lives in him. The Holy Spirit works as a type of built-in global positioning system (GPS). He speaks to your spirit only when the step you're on needs further information to guide you to the next step that is ordered or to offer comfort that you have reached your destination. The ordered steps to purpose or process do not prevent us from entering storms or troubled times, but rather they are used to show us more fully who we are in God by His grace. When the Holy Spirit is working as a GPS, it facilitates the process of getting to the stuff or down to the core of what we are really made of. Often we don't understand our substance or our core until we go through some kind of tough experience that truly exposes our identity. This process is what transforms the mindset of the 21st century virgin into a bride of Christ. It requires the cutting away of the spiritual foreskin that separates her from having an intimate relationship with God through Jesus Christ.

Followers cannot come into their true purpose with a mindset of the 21st century virgin but have to be transformed into new creations through Christ as His bride. However, God sees the relationship among the mindset of the 21st century virgins as equally important to their relationship with the bride of Christ. God waits patiently for His people to find Him. Although He is omnipresent, people still often find it challenging to find God, especially when faced with adversity. God cannot be found by the normal means we use for search and rescue. He is not just a life jacket thrown to us when we are drowning in turbulent water. But rather in the stillness of prayer and worship, we truly discover the majesty of God within us in the midst of turbulent water. The mindset of the bride of Christ uses true worship to confront challenges, seeing them as labor pains while taking deep breaths of God's perfect peace. The understanding is that suffering is only for a season and that delivery is coming soon.

In our relationship with God, we begin to know Him as the one source that creates resources. When we pray, it is a form of communication

A CHANGED MINDSET

with Him. When we pray with Him, our thought process finds rest in Him. Our conversations with God draw us to our purpose and to the plans He has for us in partnership with the Trinity. When we pray, Jesus and the Holy Spirit intercede for us and foster a conversation with the Father. We as followers may be in the presence of God from time to time and still not be empowered to have a conversation with God. To have a true conversation with the Trinity is to be in alignment with God's thought process. The Trinity has a conversation on our behalf because at times we do not know what to pray for. God wants everyone to see and understand who they are in His eyes. God wants His followers to have the same thoughts concerning the steps, plans, callings, and purpose He has for them. The mindset of the bride of Christ has conversations with God rather than to God because their thought process is aligned with His Word.

Just as worship is done in spirit and in truth, we serve God in the same way, making it so important that our minds are transformed into a like mind of Jesus Christ. Romans 7:25 says, "I thank God—through Jesus Christ our Lord! So then, with the mind I myself serve the law of God, but with the flesh the law of sin." As followers, we need to search not only to know God's voice but also to recognize His presence in our everyday lives—to have a conversation with God about the things that bring Him pleasure. The things that bring God pleasure is anything rooted in the substance where faith lives, moves, and has its being. Faith grounds God's every word, and when the mindset of the bride of Christ Jesus has a conversation with Him, it stems from His love language. Faith is one of God's love languages that His bride has learned to master. "But without faith it is impossible to please him: for he that cometh to God must believe that he is, and that he is a rewarder of them that diligently seek him" (Heb. 11:6-7 KJV).

As followers develop the mindset of the bride of Christ, they begin to collaborate with the Holy Spirit. The union that exists between Jesus and His followers helps them see adversities not as giants but as grasshoppers. That is accomplished by knowing that the greater One (Jesus) lives inside of them, and He is bigger than any adversity or challenge. But most important, God gives His followers the grace to see themselves through His eyes as even bigger giants in Jesus Christ. This new self-vision through the eyes of God brings clarity to all situations. It allows a new appreciation of every past challenge as experiences that brought them closer to the mind and heart of God. On the one hand, it may seem as if we are giving up everything for Jesus, but on the other hand is the knowledge that Jesus is the source of everything, so in essence, followers are only giving back what already belongs to Him.

God waits to grant you the desires of your heart simply because you have delighted yourself in Him in the process of transformation. God always sees the end before the beginning. Followers with the mindset of the 21st century virgin may know they have been anointed as brides but not yet received their specific appointed time for change. The process of change can be confusing and challenging. The mindset of the 21st century virgin will often feel as though they are in a paradox. Feelings of this paradox can lead to confusion about understanding who you are based on how God sees you versus what the world or you say about how you look, sound, perform, write, or act, which is quite different from what Good sees. As we are changed, faith takes our thought process and behavior and aligns it with God's thoughts. "For we walk by faith, not by sight" (2 Cor. 5:7).

The process from transformation to a changed mindset can be compared to a woman who has just discovered she is pregnant. The process of walking toward destiny is similar to realizing when you are first pregnant. However, giving birth to a baby and knowing you are saved to do something takes your thought process to a whole new level in discovering your destiny or purpose. Although they share some similarity, pregnancy includes many stages that eventually lead to motherhood and a personal relationship with your child. The same concept can be applied to having an intimate, personal relationship with God through Jesus. Through various stages of growth and development, the mindset of the bride of Christ Jesus builds and increases the level of trusting God because each ordered step or level is different than the last one. The mindset of the bride of Christ Jesus cannot see all things going on inside the transformation toward change. But there is the evidence of things hoped for that gives peace in knowing with thanksgiving that God is in control. It is similar for women who are expecting. During the process, they know their baby is developing and growing although they can't see every step because it is a faith journey.

Being thankful in all things is to acknowledge that every day is a day the Lord has made. God already has a plan for all of us by which all our needs will be provided. Therefore, it is important to acknowledge God through thanksgiving before anything else. This form of worship acknowledges first who He is in accordance with His Word. This mindset also empowers followers to see and trust in God in their daily walk with Him. The mindset of the 21st century virgin has not yet reached this level of emotional intelligence in their relationship with Christ Jesus, which often results from seeking religious activities and not Him. In the mindset of the 21st century virgin, there is an internal connection with Jesus before transformation into the mindset of the bride of Christ. According to the online website Science, an article titled "Babies Learn to Recognize Words in the Womb" shows that unborn children can recognize certain sounds before birth, especially the voice of their mother. That kind of relationship is akin to the one we can have with Christ with the mindset of the 21st century virgin and before we are changed into the mindset of the bride of Christ Jesus. John 10:3-4 tells us, "To him the doorkeeper opens, and the sheep hear his voice; and he calls his own sheep by name and leads them out. And when he brings out his own sheep, he goes before them; and the sheep follow him, for they know his voice." This type of recognition facilitates the transformation into a mindset of the bride of Christ Jesus.

The fruit of the Spirit works hand in hand with your gifts and calling during transformation and change. However, the Holy Spirit must first receive your permission to live, move, and have its being within you. You must give Him full authority to do the will of God.

The bottom line is that you're going to have to let go of your old ways of thinking and behavior and allow God to take control. Matthew 19:29 tells us, "And everyone who has left houses or brothers or sisters

THE MINDSET THAT FEEDS

or father or mother or wife or children or lands, for My name's sake, shall receive a hundredfold, and inherit eternal life." Rather than placing your focus on what you are leaving behind, pray with Jesus to open up your eyes to what God has in store. You will be called to love the unlovable, to experience joy instead of self-pity, and to foster and encourage peace when you want to wage war. You will be called to run a race that's set before you with endurance, although at times your mind and body may want to quit. Faith, meekness, self-control, and trusting God who is in control are keys to winning the race. The passion to seek the Lord will grow during the process of running the race. Learning how to apply the fruits of the Spirit is an ongoing process in this race that requires crucifying the flesh and saying yes to Jesus.

Galatians 5:24 says, "And those *who are* Christ's have crucified the flesh with its passions and desires." During this letting-go-and-letting-God process, there is a decreasing of self and an increasing of Jesus within you. The mindset of the 21st century virgin often gets stuck in the cycle of religious activity after salvation and becomes a barrier to her own emotional intelligence in having an intimate, personal relationship with Christ. The things the virgin learns along the way during the pursuit of having an intimate relationship with Jesus Christ brings it to the next level—from milk to meat. When we as followers submit our will to the Holy Spirit, His fruits become gifts we can give each other as opposed to a normal reactionary behavior. Proverbs 25:21–22 teaches, "If your enemy is hungry, give him bread to eat; and if he is thirsty, give him water to drink; for so you will heap coals of fire on his head, and the LORD will reward you." God's grace allows for this transformation and gives us the strength we need to increase into His glory.

> *And if Christ is in you, the body is dead because of sin, but the Spirit is life because of righteousness. But if the Spirit of Him who raised Jesus from the dead dwells in you, He who raised Christ from the dead will also give life to your mortal bodies through His Spirit who dwells in you. Therefore, brethren, we are debtors—not to the flesh, to live according*

A CHANGED MINDSET

to the flesh. For if you live according to the flesh you will die; but if by the Spirit you put to death the deeds of the body, you will live.

—Rom. 8:10–13

At each level, there is a further decreasing of self. There will be moments when you want to do the right thing, but that evil inclination is present within you. That is when God employs His mercy and grace to give you the strength you need to get back on the right track and press on. It is most reassuring to know that having the Spirit of Christ Jesus abiding in you gives followers the power to know and understand that they are crying for the right reasons. He offers you peace and blessed assurance during times of unanswered questions. Even Paul recalled periods of his life when he felt he could only dimly see the plans God had for him. The more you expect Jesus to reveal Himself to you, the more clearly the vision comes. Ultimately, you will move on from debating whether you should allow Him to increase in you to fully surrendering to God's will and purpose for your life. Your present situation may be uncomfortable, but God is working so a new level of explanation will be made clear.

When unexpected challenges arise, it is often God working on something much better that will take us to the next level. Jesus wants to give us His very best if we only stop settling for less than what He is offering. He offers an abundant life filled with His riches and all the desires of our hearts if we only accept His simple conditions. Our world gives us terms and conditions each day, so ask yourself who you wish to serve. Your life is so much bigger than your struggles. Try to imagine flying in an airplane, watching the ground become more and more distant as you ascend higher into the air. The same thing happens when your intimate, personal relationship with Christ is elevated and all those challenges you lived with become smaller and smaller. It's the same mindset David had when he killed Goliath; it's the same mindset of Joshua and Caleb when they reported on the land of Canaan. What God has in store for you is so much bigger than what you originally guessed or thought possible.

THE MINDSET THAT FEEDS

We are called to face unexpected challenges while accepting that the battle is not ours but God's. God puts us in circumstances that are challenging so we can produce bigger and better fruit. These challenges are good seeds planted in our souls. It is not the devil but God who gives us challenges to increase our emotional intelligence. Peace be with you as you keep in mind that you can build only what God has created you to build. We are designed to overcome all adversity because our Creator has given us that very purpose.

The God we serve is the God of creativity and purpose. He has already made plans concerning each of our destinies and given us Jesus as our daily bread. The provisions we are given each day were created to match the purpose God has given us. Everything has forethought. Psalm 118:24 proclaims, "This is the day the LORD has made; we will rejoice and be glad in it." That proclamation empowers us to worship God and be glad in our faith. We as believers rejoice that God has made us and has taken into consideration all the provisions we need to allow us to reach our destinies. Followers of Jesus are given the faith to know that all things work for good for those who are called according to God's purpose.

Faith plays a huge role for believers to know each day in their hearts that the Lord prearranged every circumstance to be worked out for His glory and for their good. That is why God instructs His followers by faith to rejoice and be glad each day. This thought process empowers followers to actively worship God and acknowledge Him as the Creator and the One who planned everything in advance for their benefit. The work God has done to prepare your day and the steps He has ordered are custom made to fit you. "And He said to me, 'My grace is sufficient for you, for My strength is made perfect in weakness.' Therefore most gladly I will rather boast in my infirmities, that the power of Christ may rest upon me. Therefore I take pleasure in infirmities, in reproaches, in needs, in persecutions, in distresses, for Christ's sake. For when I am weak, then I am strong" (2 Cor. 12:9–10).

Growing up as a young adult whose mother was known for her soul food, I could not turn food into a gourmet succulent dish if I tried. It was very frustrating for me because I love to eat food that tastes good,

A CHANGED MINDSET

and I lived all my life in a home where food was spot on and left very little room for improvement. Then I had my own family in my own home, cooking for my children and husband. My only desire was for them to enjoy the fullness of what I prepared for them to eat. For a long time it was very difficult for me to accept why failures were important in preparing the best meals my family now enjoys. The process reminds me so much of a scene from the 2005 movie *The Karate Kid*. The kid's instructor, who took a whole summer to begin training him, just made him paint stuff and wax his car. The karate kid could not understand how waxing a car (wax on, wax off) could lead him to mastering his craft. My failed attempts time after time in preparing meals for my family was a process God used to teach me how failures are tools used for success (wax on, wax off). What do failed attempts to cook for my family have anything to do with my wanting to cook the best meal for my family? What does wax on, wax off have to do with learning to master a skill in karate? It has everything to do with it. God teaches His people in a unique way how falling down and getting up just to fall down again and get up are often used to help followers master the gift God gave them for His purpose and glory.

The more you know God personally through Jesus, the more you will be able to love Him with all of your heart, soul, and mind. Transformation into the changed mindset of the bride of Christ Jesus lets followers know God intimately as the Creator of life and the source of all prosperity. He promises a path of righteousness through the blood of Jesus by giving us the steps that lead us to our destiny. As followers, we cannot naturally see the steps He has created, but in His Word, He does tell us that He is leading us on to fulfill our purpose by giving us our daily bread and preparing our path. When we look through God's eyes, we see each day loaded with victory, which empowers us to want to rejoice and be glad in it.

Deuteronomy 1:8 tells us, "See, I have set the land before you; go in and possess the land which the LORD swore to your fathers—to Abraham, Isaac, and Jacob—to give to them and their descendants after them." God instructs us to rejoice in the challenges He gives us. We must fully appreciate God as the designer, maker, and builder of each day, covered in the warranty of the blood of Jesus Christ. Being glad in the day is to be glad in Jesus, believing He is the only source to provide all the resources we need. God wants us to know who He is through His Son, our provider, healer, restorer, and shepherd. Knowing God through in an intimate, personal relationship with Jesus is a supernatural weapon that can be used to protect us daily. We can proclaim all day, "This is the day the Lord has made; we will rejoice and be glad in it." However, it is not until we know God personally in the trials, tests, and adversities that we can really rejoice.

Chapter 11

JESUS, THE CHURCH, AND RELIGION'S ACTIVITIES

You need your body to move from one place to another in order to accomplish your physical goals, but you also need your body to fulfill your spiritual purpose here on earth. The church as the body of Christ on earth serves a purpose. This purpose is more than just offering a road to salvation; it is to lead others who know they are saved to do something. The purpose of transforming the mindset of the 21st century virgin into the mindset of the bride of Christ is to teach followers to seek the kingdom of God after salvation. Salvation may be the necessary foundation that supports the church, but purpose takes followers into the heart of God so they may know His will for them. It is God's intention for believers to become doers. If faith without works is dead, then obtaining salvation without seeking the kingdom of heaven is like traveling down a dead-end street.

An intimate relationship with Jesus is what equips the mindset of the bride of Christ with the tools to make seeking the kingdom of heaven a reality. The church is a type of teacher that prepares its members to develop a personal relationship with Jesus and foster the transformation of the mindset of the 21st century virgin. By faith, the process of transformation and change occurs from a follower's personal,

A CHANGED MINDSET

intimate relationship with Jesus, including life experiences, trials, and revelation by the Holy Spirit.

As a child growing up in New York, I recall several neighborhood convenience stores that carried everyday essential items. But shopping at a Walmart Supercenter means having the opportunity to purchase everything you need—not just the bare necessities—in one place. Too often, the mindset of the 21st century virgin shops around at different emotional religious convenience stores. They look for whatever fits their needs as opposed to shopping at a Walmart Supercenter. A Walmart Supercenter represents followers getting everything they need by having a personal, intimate relationship with God. Having a well-developed, personal relationship with God through Christ is more efficient and cost-effective when acquiring major items for our spiritual development. The neighborhood emotional, religious convenience stores serve a purpose, and we need to support them, but we must remember that we need to "shop big" for our intimate, personal relationship with the mindset of the bride of Christ. Neighborhood convenience stores give us the basics before we reach our true purpose.

Jesus proclaims to us that He is the life and the resurrection. Some of us give Him 10 percent of our resources and turn to the world to make up the difference, but we often find we can't make ends meet. Jesus, who is the life and the resurrection, teaches that it is better for our sake to give Him all of ourselves because He alone holds the strategies to overcome obstacles that lead to our purpose. He is our ultimate Walmart Supercenter, and the final product is having an intimate relationship with the One who is the source of all blessings. Jesus is everything we need, including the wisdom we need to live well in this life and the life to come. In knowing Him, we find an understanding of how to meet all of life's challenges. He is the Alpha and the Omega. Jesus is the Teacher who holds the tests of life in one hand and the answers in the other. He can walk on water and command the wind and the waves to be still. He is our rest in times of trouble. He is the source who meets all our needs and makes all resources available to us.

God caused Adam, the first man, to fall asleep and then pulled out of Adam everything he would need in a perfect mate. There are countless others in the Bible who had a Walmart Supercenter shopping experience with God when they were given everything they needed to make them whole. When Jesus connected with the woman at the well and the woman who had a blood disorder for 12 years, He gave them what they needed by becoming a source of what they needed to change their life forever and not a resource for just that season of their life.

> *I am the true vine, and My Father is the vinedresser. Every branch in Me that does not bear fruit He takes away; and every* branch *that bears fruit He prunes, that it may bear more fruit. You are already clean because of the word, which I have spoken to you. Abide in Me, and I in you. As the branch cannot bear fruit of itself, unless it abides in the vine, neither can you, unless you abide in Me. I am the vine, you* are *the branches. He who abides in Me, and I in him, bears much fruit; for without Me you can do nothing. If anyone does not abide in Me, he is cast out as a branch and is withered; and they gather them and throw* them *into the fire, and they are burned. If you abide in Me, and My words abide in you, you will ask what you desire, and it shall be done for you. By this My Father is glorified, that you bear much fruit; so you will be My disciples. As the Father loved Me, I also have loved you; abide in My love. If you keep My commandments, you will abide in My love, just as I have kept My Father's commandments and abide in His love. These things I have spoken to you, that My joy may remain in you, and* that *your joy may be full. This is My commandment, that you love one another as I have loved you. Greater love has no one than this, than to lay down one's life for his friends. You are My friends if you do whatever I command you. No longer do I call you servants, for a servant does not know what his master is doing; but I have called you friends, for all things that I heard from My Father I have made known to you. You did not choose Me, but I chose you and appointed you that you should go and bear fruit, and* that *your fruit should remain, that whatever you ask the Father in My name He may give*

> *you. These things I command you, that you love one another. If the world hates you, you know that it hated Me before it hated you. If you were of the world, the world would love its own. Yet because you are not of the world, but I chose you out of the world, therefore the world hates you. Remember the word that I said to you, "A servant is not greater than his master." If they persecuted Me, they will also persecute you. If they kept My word, they will keep yours also. But all these things they will do to you for My name's sake, because they do not know Him who sent Me. If I had not come and spoken to them, they would have no sin, but now they have no excuse for their sin. He who hates Me hates My Father also. If I had not done among them the works which no one else did, they would have no sin; but now they have seen and also hated both Me and My Father. But* this happened *that the word might be fulfilled which is written in their law, "They hated Me without a cause." But when the Helper comes, whom I shall send to you from the Father, the Spirit of truth who proceeds from the Father, He will testify of Me. And you also will bear witness, because you have been with Me from the beginning.*
> —John 15:1–27

For me, it all started when God drew me closer to Jesus through seeking first the kingdom of God and His righteousness. Originally when I started on my journey, I was seeking a God who dwelled around me. When I started to find the kingdom of God, I was touched with a revelation of who I really am in His eyes. This revelation caused me, with the mindset of a 21st century virgin, to chase after the God I never knew, the One I had always desired, the missing piece that completed who I am in the great I AM. God told Moses to tell the children of Israel "I AM WHO I AM" (Exod. 3:14).

God gave me the mindset of a bride of Christ. With this new mindset, I find myself seeking the I AM who lives in me so I can discover my purpose and live in Him. And knowing how to operate the tools He has placed in me has given me the support to find my role as His servant and His friend. Now my focus is on His kingdom and learning all I can about the great I AM to perfect myself in His Word.

> *My beloved put in his hand by the hole of the door, and my bowels were moved for him. I rose up to open to my beloved; and my hands dropped with myrrh, and my fingers with sweet-smelling myrrh upon the handles of the lock. I opened to my beloved; but my beloved had withdrawn himself, and was gone: my soul failed when he spake: I sought him, but I could not find him; I called him, but he gave me no answer. The watchmen that went about the city found me, they smote me, they wounded me; the keepers of the walls took away my veil from me. I charge you, O daughters of Jerusalem, if ye find my beloved, that ye tell him, that I am sick of love. What is thy beloved more than another beloved, O thou fairest among women? What is thy beloved more than another beloved, that thou dost so charge us? My beloved is white and ruddy, the chiefest among ten thousand. His head is as the most fine gold, his locks are bushy, and black as a raven. His eyes are as the eyes of doves by the rivers of waters, washed with milk, and fitly set. His cheeks are as a bed of spices, as sweet flowers: his lips like lilies, dropping sweet smelling myrrh. His hands are as gold rings set with the beryl: his belly is as bright ivory overlaid with sapphires. His legs are as pillars of marble, set upon sockets of fine gold: his countenance is as Lebanon, excellent as the cedars. His mouth is most sweet: yea, he is altogether lovely. This is my beloved, and this is my friend, O daughters of Jerusalem.*
> —Song of Sol. 5:4–16 KJV

Jesus is not only the gatekeeper of love from God, but He holds the key to our true purpose in Him. He is the developer and the deliverer of the mindset of the 21st century virgin mindset in becoming the bride of Christ.

Chapter 12

DELIVERY

To facilitate the delivery of your purpose, you can use worship similar to having labor pains to activate what is already inside of you. I once heard that hardships could be seen as a gift from God. As a mother who gave birth to eight babies, I always elected to participate in natural childbirth. To say the very least, the labor process was very painful in every delivery. I perceived it as a hardship and could not find an effective way to cope with the pain. I was 28 years old when I gave birth to my oldest son. The pain was so overwhelming that I attempted to bite my husband's hand so he could feel a little of the pain I was going through. Consequently, I was placed in a four-point mechanical leather restraint and was freed only after I gave birth and calmed down.

The point I am making is that it was not the intensity of the pain or that I was forced into a four-point restraint, but it was rather my inability to cope effectively with the labor process. Having given birth naturally several times has taught me so much about the labor and delivery process. I eventually learned how to cope by working with the labor pain and not against it. The ability to give birth comes with various levels of discomfort and pain for many women. But needless to say, giving birth is a miracle and a gift of life.

A CHANGED MINDSET

By my eighth child, I knew what to expect during childbirth and had a much better understanding of the importance of resting and how effective breathing facilitates self-control during contractions and produces less anxiety. Effective breathing techniques during a contraction can also increase strength and energy for both the mother and the baby. It has been noted that effective breathing can prevent the mother from pushing at the wrong time. Inexperienced mothers often have the tendency during a contraction to hold their breath when the pain level increases, but proper breathing helps women focus on the contractions as a productive part of the birthing process and not the intensity of the pain. Another goal of breathing exercises is to promote relaxation during labor.

God used my deliveries to demonstrate how worship can be an effective tool when dealing with struggles. Worship reminds us of His presence and the perfect peace we have when our mind is stayed on Him. Worship is expressing, acknowledging, and knowing who God is. This knowledge empowers the mindset of the 21st century virgin to propel into the transformation process in changing to a mindset of the bride of Christ. This process of transformation ultimately gives God His glory. Everything God allows to happen is part of a strategic plan to foster His relationship with His followers, which results in a mindset that has moved from transformation to a changed mindset. Since the very beginning of time, God has wanted a personal relationship with all of creation through Jesus Christ.

Knowing who God is and where He is in challenging situations promotes a sense of perfect peace. Effective breathing is helpful when coping with various types of pain, anxiety, and fear, and so is worship. Followers who have the mindset of the bride of Christ Jesus are more apt to use worship during difficult challenges. They are equipped to use worship when experiencing challenges similar to contractions that often lead to delivery. Worship is like an effective breathing technique; it reminds us that what we are going through will not last forever. When coping with pain, worship can promote relaxation as we are reminded that Christ Jesus is everything we need. James 1:2–5 tells us, "My brethren,

DELIVERY

count it all joy when you fall into various trials, knowing that the testing of your faith produces patience. But let patience have *its* perfect work, that you may be perfect and complete, lacking nothing. If any of you lacks wisdom, let him ask of God, who gives to all liberally and without reproach, and it will be given to him." If we really understand how God relates to us through His Word, we can better grasp the meaning behind trials and tribulations in our lives and how He molds and reshapes us into a whole person from the transformation process to a changed mindset. Therefore, challenging times or adversities can be seen as gifts from God used to facilitate change.

In the Gospel of John, sisters Mary and Martha bury their brother Lazarus. These sisters were great friends of Jesus, and their brother was especially loved by Him. Jesus knew that Lazarus was very ill, but His response to this was that God will be glorified through his illness. Jesus intentionally did not visit Lazarus for two days. After those two days, He decided to go to Judea even though His disciples did not want Him to go for fear that He might be killed. Thomas and the other disciples who came with Him to Judea were willing to follow Christ, even if they were to die alongside Him. Jesus explained to the disciples that when you walk in the light, even during difficult times, you will not stumble. It is only when you walk in darkness that you could stumble. Jesus told them that it was time to visit their friend Lazarus in his sleep. Of course, His disciples found that Lazarus was sleeping in the sleep of death and did not understand that Jesus wanted to raise him up for God's glory. When they arrived, Lazarus had already been in his grave four days. Martha received news that Jesus was on His way and left the house to go greet Him. "Then said Martha unto Jesus, 'Lord, if thou hadst been here, my brother had not died'" (John 11:21 KJV). These words remind us of the many moments when we have all asked God, "Hey, what happened? Did you fall asleep? Were you not watching? If you were paying attention, this would not have happened. Didn't you hear our call for help?"

There is no doubt that the love Jesus had for Martha, Mary, and Lazarus is the same love He has for His followers, and especially those with the mindset of the 21st century virgin. We often find ourselves

A CHANGED MINDSET

asking God questions out of ignorance, pride, anger, confusion, pain, or feelings of hopelessness. Mary and Martha were filled with so many of those questions, yet they understood that Jesus is the answer to life-and-death questions. They knew that Jesus would raise Lazarus from the dead on the last day when He told Martha, "I am the resurrection, and the life: he that believeth in me, though he were dead, yet shall he live; and whosoever lives and believeth in me shall never die" (John 11:25–26). Jesus comes to us to answer our cries of despair; however, He sometimes answers them by way of the process. Mary and Martha told Jesus that their brother Lazarus would not have died had He been there, implying that He had come too late, but since He is omnipresent and not limited by time, that is impossible. Jesus is only subject to the will of His heavenly Father. A day and a thousand years may be the same span of time to Him. Psalm 73:26 tells us, "My flesh and my heart fail; *but* God *is* the strength of my heart and my portion forever."

Walking with Jesus supports a good alignment in the mindset of the bride of Christ, although it has its challenges. Our perception of life or our mindset as it relates to our fellowship with Christ can shake or shape our faith. How we choose to think governs the actions we take. In his letters to the Corinthians, Paul tells of a treasure we all have inside us that keeps us from feelings of bewilderment and helps us cope with difficulties. At times, life's pressures can be viewed as storms with troubled waters on the rise. It is easy for our faith to become weak in these situations and to feel like we may slip under the waves. This feeling of imminent drowning makes you want to quit, but through His grace and mercy, God will bring you through and will not allow any outside pressure to break you. It is love that produces a fertile ground in which faith can develop and mature. The more intimate and personal your relationship with God is, the more your faith will develop. A 21st century virgin mindset will ask God for an increase of faith. The bride of Christ will look for ways to know Jesus at His core in every situation by faith.

Through His love, God gives us grace, which is the source of our strength and ability to endure. His grace is power and the light at the end of a dark tunnel. His grace keeps us steadfast and able to withstand any storm. His grace allows us to come to Him with boldness and make our requests known to Him.

> "The glory of the LORD shall be revealed, and all flesh shall see it together; for the mouth of the LORD has spoken." The voice said, "Cry out!" And he said, "What shall I cry?" "All flesh is grass, and all its loveliness is like the flower of the field. The grass withers, the flower fades, because the breath of the LORD blows upon it; surely the people are grass. The grass withers, the flower fades, but the word of our God stands forever." O Zion, you who bring good tidings, get up into the high mountain; O Jerusalem, you who bring good tidings, lift up your voice with strength, lift it up, be not afraid; say to the cities of Judah, "Behold your God!"
> —Isa. 40:5–9

Isaiah 40:31 says, "But those who wait on the LORD shall renew *their* strength; they shall mount up with wings like eagles, they shall run and not be weary, they shall walk and not faint." God knows everything we have been through, are going through, and are yet to experience. He is our yesterday, our today, and our tomorrow. He is God! We have no authority but through Him. We cannot make the moon change its course or control the tides; we cannot change the color of our skin or keep a star from falling; but we can gain an understanding of God who controls all things. In this fast-paced age, phrases such as "perfect peace" and "be still and know that I am God" are rare to experience. With our current 21st century virgin attitude, we usually ask questions such as "what have you done for me lately?" Seeking riches from the world with a sense of entitlement does not prepare you for life's adversities. Being self-centered ultimately leads to self-destruction. When forced to confront life's disappointments and pain, many of us react rather than respond. When Mary and Martha were weeping, Jesus groaned in His spirit and was troubled by their reaction to their brother's death. Jesus wept because of His love of Lazarus and his family.

A CHANGED MINDSET

Like Mary and so many others, we look only enough to see the surface but not enough to know Him at His core. We as followers seek Him out and even go so far as to say we love God, but rarely do we really worship Him for who He is. Many of us have attended church but have not allowed what He perceives as His church to be part of the way we think. But the God we serve wants us to know Him so much more and to exceed our expectations more than we can ever imagine. Jesus came on our behalf, not just for us to have life but for us to live it more abundantly. In doing so, Jesus is waiting for the mindset of the 21st century virgin to be transformed and changed to His bride. The mindset of the bride of Christ follows her bridegroom simply because there is an alignment to His thoughts. The desire of wanting to know who Jesus is at His core moves the mindset of the bride of Christ to seek first the kingdom of heaven and its righteousness. The mindset of the bride of Christ allows followers to expand their desire in seeking an intimate and personal relationship with God through Jesus rather than depending on other people or organizations to do it for them. There comes a time in every follower's spiritual development when you stop drinking milk and start eating meat from the king's table. The difference between the 10 virgins parable in Matthew 25:1–13 is that one group of virgins already had what they needed to move forward and meet their groom, and the others did not because they were not aligned in preparation for the groom's return.

In his letter to the Philippians, Paul says, "Not that I have already attained, or am already perfected; but I press on, that I may lay hold of that for which Christ Jesus has also laid hold of me. Brethren, I do not count myself to have apprehended; but one thing *I do*, forgetting those things which are behind and reaching forward to those things which are ahead" (Phil. 3:12–13). To know Jesus is to know that He is the giver of life and the reason we live. He came that we may have life through Him and have it more abundantly, which comes through knowledge of Him. Those who walked with Him and loved Him knew that He was the Son of God and that on the last day, the children of the Lord would rise and enter the kingdom of heaven. Yet they couldn't see or understand, even at that time, that the kingdom of God was already right in front of them. Jesus told us then and tells us today that He and the Father are one. "But seek ye first the kingdom of God and His righteousness, and all these things shall be added to you" (Matt. 6:33). The abundant life God wants for us lies in understanding the kingdom of heaven and realizing that the treasures are the lessons learned in the journey of seeking Him. The mindset of the bride of Christ Jesus is empowered through the process of going through a test, not just having the knowledge, and then passing that test.

Passing the test doesn't prove you've learned anything; however, the work you put in before taking the test is the evidence of the things you learned. Having the ability to see the kingdom of heaven is the evidence of the hard work you put in during your intimate, personal time with Jesus. How often are the kingdom of God and His righteousness so close to us but we fail to see them? His kingdom is at our fingertips, but a mindset that has not been changed into a mindset of the bride of Christ Jesus may keep us from finding it. Understanding His kingdom is impossible for us to do alone, which is why God sent His Son. Jesus holds the key that unlocks the door to the kingdom of God. Jesus came for those with the 21st century virgin mindset that they may be transformed into the bride of Christ. Jesus became our first example of living life on purpose and a road map in seeking the kingdom of God as we come to know our purpose.

In John 11:14–15 (NIV) we read, "So then he told them plainly, 'Lazarus is dead, and for your sake I am glad I was not there, so that you may believe. But let us go to him.'" Lazarus' state was not the point Jesus wanted to get across. Rather He wanted those present to know that trusting Him is a daily faith walk. The transformation from the mindset of the 21st century virgin into the mindset of the bride of Christ will manifest itself as we become more and more spiritually connected with Jesus. As a result, followers will be empowered to see His perfect peace because of their knowledge of Him, even in the midst of life's raging storms.

In the book of Matthew, we read about the disciples being concerned about a furious storm when they were in a boat on the Sea of Galilee.

A CHANGED MINDSET

Jesus was sleeping peacefully during the storm and woke up to find His disciples in a state of panic. It wasn't the storm that awoke Jesus but rather His disciples' lack of faith. As His followers, we often find ourselves in similar circumstances when we exhibit a lack of faith. In troubled times, our human nature kicks in, and we hold on to what we experience with our five senses and abandon the certainty of faith. During Jesus's visit to Capernaum, a centurion told him about one of his servants who was very ill. "And Jesus saith unto him, I will come and heal him. The centurion answered and said, Lord, I am not worthy that thou shouldest come under my roof: but speak the word only, and my servant shall be healed" (Matt. 8:7–9 KJV). This centurion understood the power behind words because he was a man with authority. With a word, he could bid his servants to come or go and do as he pleased. Jesus was so amazed by the faith of this man that He said to His followers that He had never met a man in Israel with such great faith. The centurion was under the influence of the Holy Spirit, and as a result, he was able to capture the substance of who Jesus is at His core. He spoke Jesus's love language and believed that Jesus is the substance that faith is made of. The cure for his servant was what the centurion hoped for. Because he knew who Jesus is at His core, Jesus didn't have to come to his house to heal his servant. He knew that if Jesus would just speak a word, that alone would be enough for his servant to be healed. The centurion saw in his thought process that Jesus was the source of faith and His word an extension of it. It is in this mindset of the bride of Christ Jesus that Jesus is the author and finisher of their faith, and His Word is the extension of things hoped for.

The love the centurion had for his servant impressed Jesus. In this example, we see how the love that motivated the centurion's faith was so strong that it became a game-changer in how the servant would be healed. In fact, this example of love is similar to the love God has for the world—a love so great that He sent His Son as His living Word from heaven so His followers might have the right to eternal life. Jesus told the centurion, "Go your way; and as you have believed, *so* let it be done for you" (Matt 8:13). The centurion's servant was immediately healed.

What is it about this centurion or the Canaanite woman begging Jesus to heal her daughter that caused Jesus to take notice? Could it be their demonstration of a love so great for someone else that they were willing to leave their homes in hopes of finding deliverance through Jesus, the author and finisher of their faith? It does appear that they all shared a type of love that would merit God's love for the world.

Jesus can be standing next to you, but nothing will change until He is fully revealed through your love for God. Through Him you become a champion over your own challenges. In my experience, challenges bring out two qualities in people. Challenges either motivate people to become champions or give them an excuse to never know what they are really made of. Love often motivates faith into applying action. In the book of Matthew, Jesus teaches that if we have faith as small as a mustard seed, it will be enough for us to move a mountain. Everything becomes possible. In the book of John, Jesus tells His disciples that they may do greater works when they believe. If we understand this concept, then seeking the kingdom of God becomes less challenging. But none of this is possible unless love is the motivator in seeking the kingdom of heaven and the heart of God. All these things, including faith and hope, will fall into place when love has taken its rightful place. "And now abideth faith, hope, charity, these three; but the greatest of these is charity" (1 Cor. 13:13 KJV).

Jesus said that He is the vine and we are the branches. With Him we produce much fruit, and without Him we are incapable of producing anything promising. God has designed an individual plan for each of His children to find their purpose. These plans, or ordered steps, allow us to prosper; they give us hope and are the blueprints we need to discover our true potential. We should no longer ask if Christ fits into our agenda; we should ask how we fit into Christ's agenda in finding purpose. In this process of transformation, a changed mindset of the bride of Christ supports the beautiful feet of the gospel of Jesus Christ.

Chapter 13

BEAUTIFUL FEET

The beautiful feet of the mindset of the bride of Christ bring healing to the world. The kingdom of heaven is the place where God and your perception or thought process of Him become more aligned to His thought process. When you walk into a room in a difficult circumstance, the kingdom of God continues to remain with you. His presence takes over all circumstances simply because as a bride of Christ, the greater One lives within you. The huge advantage to having the mindset of a bride of Christ as opposed to the mindset of a 21st century virgin is how every outcome is based on the relationship you have with God instead of reacting to challenging situations. The feet of the bride of Christ are beautiful because they carry the Word of God. God's Word brings hope and healing to those who have not discovered their relationship with Him. The mindset of the bride of Christ Jesus loves to sit at the feet of who Jesus Christ is.

Reflexology teaches that your feet are a conduit to major organs of the body. This form of holistic care can be defined as a natural healing art grounded in the concept that reflexes in the feet, hands, ears, and other parts of the body are associated with glands and organs within the body. By applying pressure on these body parts, circulation is increased, and stress can be released from the various internal organs. If reflexology can heal the body through the feet, then it makes sense that caring for the spiritual feet of others would help heal the body of Christ. Having your feet washed spiritually can help remove the cares of the world and any negative dust or dirt picked up along the way. Washing the feet of others also demonstrates effective leadership skills and can help followers continue in their work for Christ. Jesus is the living Word of God, created to be our first human example of what we need to become as followers. Even though He has cleansed our sins by His blood during His crucifixion, we still need our feet washed daily to help us wash off the dirt picked up during our travels in life. God's purpose for His children is for us to care for one another spiritually, washing others' feet as an act of care and love. There are many ways to wash people's feet. We can actively listen to them after they have undergone a challenging journey. Another one way is to offer a word of encouragement or demonstrate the fruit of the Spirit. God wants us to have a servant's mentality so He can use us to fulfill His plan and support one another in pursuing His Son. Jesus is our example of how to be an optimal leader through servitude. As His elect, we are joined in Him as one; we are called to serve Him by serving others. When we spiritually wash the feet of others, it's an opportunity for them to give God His glory.

The Bible tells us there is a balm in Gilead to heal sick souls. The mindset of the bride of Christ is that balm to heal the sick and wash the feet of our neighbors as they go about the work of the Lord. You would be surprised at the number of times God gives us opportunities—opportunities we miss—to wash the feet of others. The Good Samaritan is a wonderful example of someone who spiritually washed someone's feet. Like the Good Samaritan, the mindset of the bride of Christ edifies, builds up, and supports the body of Christ in washing the feet of others. It is the greatest act of service we can do for someone else, and it truly builds up the church as the body of Christ. You never know who you may encounter during your travels and who you may come across that need their spiritual feet washed. When we wash the feet of others, we are in many cases offering a type of balm that can heal their pain or their sick soul.

With the balm of Gilead, there is healing and a shelter from the rain. There is power in the love demonstrated in washing the feet of others. If we have not tapped into this power source yet, it is time to gain access. Through the fruit of the Holy Spirit, we are empowered to use our gifts to serve and wash the feet of others and are empowered to do great acts for one another. "But the fruit of the Spirit is love, joy, peace, forbearance, kindness, goodness, faithfulness, gentleness and self-control. Against such things there is no law. Those who belong to Christ Jesus have crucified the flesh with its passions and desires" (Gal. 5:22–24 NIV). Since we live by the Spirit, let us keep in step with the Spirit, giving the Holy Spirit permission to function as our chief operating engineer.

> *The* Lord *is my shepherd; I shall not want. He makes me to lie down in green pastures; He leads me beside the still waters. He restores my soul; He leads me in the paths of righteousness for His name's sake. Yea, though I walk through the valley of the shadow of death, I will fear no evil; for You are with me; Your rod and Your staff, they comfort me. You prepare a table before me in the presence of my enemies; You anoint my head with oil; my cup runs over. Surely goodness and mercy shall follow me all the days of my life; and I will dwell in the house of the* Lord *forever.*
> —Ps. 23:1–6

When we allow Jesus to be the Lord of our lives, He becomes the Good Shepherd who leads us to green pastures. These pastures can be medicine for the soul that takes the form of chastisements, trials, and tribulations; they are not always pleasant, but not everything that helps us grow appears joyful at the start. Green pastures are a resting place in the arms of Jesus. We may be met with difficult times, but they are designed to bring out the very best in us. That is when we are remolded and our destiny is shaped. Green pastures are ordered to bring us to the next level of faith and give us better insight and preparation for future challenges. Jesus uses the rod and staff to guide us in this new direction because, just like sheep, we often tend to wander off in different directions.

A CHANGED MINDSET

We are told that Christ has prepared a table for us in the presence of our enemies. There will come a day that everything that once held us down will be a footstool that serves us. While you may feel you have lost the battle, the Lord is preparing to restore your soul. He will renew your faith in Him. Your victory has already been established.

> *The hand of the* LORD *came upon me and brought me out in the Spirit of the* LORD, *and set me down in the midst of the valley; and it* was *full of bones. Then He caused me to pass by them all around, and behold,* there were *very many in the open valley; and indeed* they were *very dry. And He said to me,* "Son of man, can these bones live?" *So I answered,* "O Lord GOD, You know." *Again He said to me,* "Prophesy to these bones, and say to them, 'O dry bones, hear the word of the* LORD! *Thus says the Lord* GOD *to these bones: "Surely I will cause breath to enter into you, and you shall live. I will put sinews on you and bring flesh upon you, cover you with skin and put breath in you; and you shall live. Then you shall know that I am* the LORD."' *So I prophesied as I was commanded; and as I prophesied, there was a noise, and suddenly a rattling; and the bones came together, bone to bone. Indeed, as I looked, the sinews and the flesh came upon them, and the skin covered them over; but* there was no *breath in them. Also He said to me,* "Prophesy to the breath, prophesy, son of man, and say to the breath, 'Thus says the Lord* GOD: *"Come from the four winds, O breath, and breathe on these slain, that they may live."'" *So I prophesied as He commanded me, and breath came into them, and they lived, and stood upon their feet, an exceedingly great army.*
> —Ezek 37:1–10

When faced with dilemmas, at times followers see them like a sea of dead bones. It could be a challenge with your health, family, society, job, church, home, or more. But the Holy Spirit will lead you in a direction that will give you the sustaining power you need. God's breath is His Word, which cannot fail but brings forth life. His Word never has insufficient funds and never bounces. It stands when everything else fails.

> *Do not remember the former things, nor consider the things of old. Behold, I will do a new thing, now it shall spring forth; shall you not know it? I will even make a road in the wilderness and rivers in the desert. The beast of the field will honor Me, the jackals and the ostriches, because I give waters in the wilderness and rivers in the desert, to give drink to My people, My chosen.*
> —Isa. 43:18–20

God will show you a new way of looking at things in a changed mindset as the bride of Christ.

This book was born from a test I went through after investing years of preparation and thousands of dollars in my education. The test or journey to further my higher education positioned me for transformation and a changed mindset. There were times when I thought working toward my nursing degree and doctorate of nursing practice was like wasting energy and money. But contrary to my original thought process of getting my doctorate, it turned out that God saw something else. Consequently, it was the process of becoming an effective learner, and faith was my teacher. God used this road and the challenges I had to face with a learning disability to get the degree. He used the ordered steps and the lessons learned along the way to prepare me for my destiny. There is something to be said that the greater the test, the greater the blessing. The lesson I learned was how faith works in a substance that has little or no chance of becoming positive or prosperous, and yet in my thinking process, I did not see the positive or that it being prosperous could not be an option. It was hope that kept me believing that nothing was impossible for God.

Reality reminded me every day of my limitations and previous failures. But God never removed my past failures, my learning disabilities, or my limitations. What God did do was change the way I thought about His Word and how I saw Him above my past failures, my learning disabilities, and my limitations. As children of God, we find ourselves reacting to two kinds of opposition. The first is when we are willing to accept the trial as part of God's perfect will for us in order to strengthen our faith in who He is. The second is when we refuse to muster up the faith we need for the trial. You are inevitably going to have difficult moments in life, but deliverance is coming. But before deliverance arrives, you must first understand that you will be going against the grain to fight for God's perfect will for your life.

In Acts 9:5, God explains to Saul that every time he moves away from God's direction for him, he is kicking against what is best for him and is hurting himself. On the foot of an ox is a sharp piece of metal that pokes the ox every time he attempts to leave the area his owner has placed him in. The more the ox is determined to fight back and kick, the deeper the puncture and the greater the suffering. It is not until the ox trusts his owner that he learns the lesson. Did your mother ever tell you that your arms are too short to box with God? This is a great opportunity to trust God and the direction He has for your life and not try to helplessly fight Him.In the book of Jonah, we read how Jonah was swallowed by a great fish and then kept in the belly for three days and three nights. Jonah reached this destiny as a result of his disobedience to the Lord and fleeing to Tarshish. He refused to go to Nineveh where God had called him to speak His Word and deliver the people out of sin and into salvation. Jonah thought the people of Nineveh were too wicked and small-minded to be moved by the Word of God. Often our perspective is limited by what we can achieve, but God asks us what we truly hope for. All things are possible in Christ Jesus who speaks life to our dry bones. Jesus stands between you and the struggles or challenges in your life that appear like dry bones. He will deliver you from your situation and restore you to victory, but it begins with a changed mindset. In 2 Corinthians 12:9, God tells us that His grace is sufficient for us. It makes us perfect and teaches us why Paul was so elated when he knew that through his weakness, the powers of Jesus Christ rested on him. Once your mind has been recalibrated to think correctly, your head will be on straight, and as a result, the rest of your body and your behavior will follow the mindset of Christ Jesus.

What I can do to please God is very simple—it's faith. It is the love of God that introduces faith as Jesus, the living Word of God and the author and finisher of our faith. "But we have this treasure in earthen vessels, that the excellence of the power may be of God, and not of us" (2 Cor. 4:7). Jesus is always a gentleman and never forces Himself on anyone. He simply knocks on the door and waits for you to open it. "Faith *comes* by hearing, and hearing from the word of God" (Rom. 10:17). Faith as small as a mustard seed can move mountains. God is revealed to His followers because of His Spirit living inside of them. Faith is everything we need to please Him. In God's Word, we can achieve all things if we first seek the kingdom of heaven and its righteousness.

I now realize how God used my disability and why I was placed in private schools. He used my limitation to learn like others and the structured learning environment to mold me for His use. He allowed my parents to place me in Catholic schools to mold me for His glory, even though it was very challenging for me. I can only imagine that it was not easy for Jesus to be the Son of God and to grow up as a carpenter's son. One of the great things about my relationship with Christ is that it is not complicated; it's simple and straightforward. The best news is that I don't have to wonder if God loves me in spite of my limitation and mistakes. I don't ever have to look over my shoulder to see if He is still there or if He has found someone better than me. Truly, my fellowship with Christ is the best personal and intimate relationship I could ever have. There are times I find myself wandering off like a lost sheep from the Good Shepherd. But thank you, Jesus. You truly are the Good Shepherd who uses His rod to redirect me and at times pull me back when necessary for my good.

In Luke 15, the woman who lost a valuable coin searched high and low until she found it. Although it was only one coin, it was enough for her to stop and search and leave nothing unturned until she found it. Followers demonstrate how important their relationship is by seeking diligently the kingdom of God and its righteousness. With the same mind that is in Christ Jesus, the bride of Christ builds an intimate and personal relationship. The closer your personal relationship is with God, the more valuable Jesus becomes to you. God sees the mindset of the 21st century virgin as a beloved member of the body of Christ who has been predestined to be transformed by a changed mindset. Even though we are challenged with barriers that interfere with building an intimate relationship with Him, God still sees each and every one of us as a potential bride.

The Holy Spirit can empower the mindset of the 21st century virgin to change the mindset from poor choices and ineffective thinking to having a mind like Christ's. In Romans 8:11, we read that the same Holy Spirit who raised Jesus from the dead lives in us. The Spirit can raise the members of the body of Jesus Christ out of sin. Jesus, our bridegroom, paid the price by becoming a living offering for our sins, which placed the church in the position to be His bride.

Lord, thank You for taking our place and becoming a much worthier sacrifice. Because of Your sacrifice, I am not limited to living within the framework of the mindset of the 21st century virgin. Through you, Lord, I can be transformed into Your bride. Jesus, Your sacrifice is more than forgiving our sins; it is also giving your bride something worthy enough to give back to God. Through Your eyes, the Son of God can be seen in Your followers, and they can boldly wear the pure white wedding gown made of chiffon and embroidered with the finest pearls, the Chantilly lace to cover the head, and a train that flows down and leaves a path for others to follow and worship His presence.

Chapter 14

A CHANGED MINDSET VIEW OF THE KINGDOM OF GOD

As followers and friends of God, we have a relationship with Him that is spot on when we seek to worship Him in every circumstance. The mindset of the bride of Christ Jesus comes to know Him by seeking first the kingdom of God. This type of mindset is where His bride worships Him for who He is and before the manifestation of what is to come. In the midst of smoke, rubbish, and uncertainty is where faith instructs followers to trust in who God says He is. The Holy Spirit teaches the mindset of the bride of Christ how to dress appropriately for change. Ephesians 6:16–17 says, "Above all, taking the shield of faith with which you will be able to quench all the fiery darts of the wicked one. And take the helmet of salvation, and the sword of the Spirit, which is the word of God."

When God reveals your gift or calling, He will at times use the adversary to motivate you toward destiny. The adversary can work for your good by putting you in circumstances that leave you tapping into the core of who God is inside of you. You will know that you've arrived at the kingdom of heaven when you want for nothing more than

A CHANGED MINDSET

to know who God is at His core. Knowing who God is at His core is seeking first the kingdom of God. It is at this time that the Holy Spirit reveals God's Word planted inside of you before your mother ever met your father. It is this Word planted inside of you that speaks life to your dry bones. His Word will never return to him void or with insufficient funds. The gifts you have are bigger and more valuable than anything you can manage on your own. Reaching the core of who God is through Jesus empowers followers to know who they are and know their source of strength. Once you know who God is at His core, you will have the ability to leave everything behind for Him. Seeking first the kingdom God and its righteous reveals who God is, but it also reveals what He sees in you. All these things and provisions are what God has for those with a mindset of the bride of Christ Jesus as they live life with purpose. As you seek first the kingdom of God, everything you need for what God purposes you to be has already been added to you without asking. Every provision needed in order for the mindset of the bride of Christ Jesus to be purpose-driven is marked for success.

In Mark 10:29–31, we read, "So Jesus answered and said, 'Assuredly, I say to you, there is no one who has left house or brothers or sisters or father or mother or wife or children or lands, for My sake and the gospel's, who shall not receive a hundredfold now in this time—houses and brothers and sisters and mothers and children and lands, with persecutions—and in the age to come, eternal life.'" Only through giving up all, as Jesus instructs us, are we empowered to chase after the One who is responsible for creating all things, including purpose. To follow God, we have to worship Him in spirit so He may be revealed to us in our minds by His Spirit. To be detached from the body is to be present with the Lord. Fasting is one form of detachment from the body and subjecting to the Spirit. The body has no domain in gaining access to the kingdom of God. His kingdom is with us because it is the place where God takes up His residency. Because He is omnipresent, followers can worship Him anywhere and gain access to Him. As followers, we have to learn to trust God every step of the way. Our faith should not be founded on our emotions but rather on his infallible Word.

A CHANGED MINDSET VIEW OF THE KINGDOM OF GOD

It is more valuable to see God as a healer than to just be healed. Many people are healed, but not many recognize God as their healer when they are still waiting to be healed. The woman who lived with the blood disorder for 12 years approached Jesus not merely to be healed but to be made whole. She saw Him as her healer before she got healed. Although she was tired, broken, and discouraged, her faith was in knowing that who He is was the strength that moved her to touch the hem of His garment. At times when we are sick or broken, we see healing as the only answer when God really wants to draw us closer to Him and make us whole through His Son. Knowing what pleases God fosters a closer relationship with Jesus. He is the substance of faith and the evidence of our deepest desires.

The kingdom of heaven is not just a place but a mindset that empowers the bride of Christ. Everything that is valuable to God is from the kingdom and manifested in our natural world. It is important that the mindset of the 21st century virgin be transformed so the mindset of those individuals can see and embrace the process toward purpose. The mindset of the 21st century virgin often seeks after the presence of Jesus in religious activities when He is waiting for her at the well. At this waiting place, Jesus offers rivers of living water in exchange for renouncing the old way of thinking. God sees His bride as a citizen of His kingdom and not as a worldly citizen. Seeking first the kingdom of heaven creates a type of thinking that empowers the bride of Christ to think like Him. It is through this type of thinking that the mindset of the bride of Christ Jesus develops kingdom concept while living in the natural. This mindset reflects the things that are important to God.

"Do not lay up for yourselves treasures on earth, where moth and rust destroy and where thieves break in and steal; but lay up for yourselves treasures in heaven, where neither moth nor rust destroys and where thieves do not break in and steal. For where your treasure is, there your heart will be also" (Matt. 6:19–21). The kingdom of heaven is not just a place but a mindset that empowers the bride of Christ's thought process. Anything of great significance to God comes from His kingdom first and then is manifested in the natural. God has implemented kingdom concepts and principles seeded in our thinking to influence others to live life and to have it more abundantly. This way of thinking reflects Jesus's knowledge and understanding of who God is. Seeking first the kingdom of God and its righteousness is to know the personal thoughts of God and the revelation of His thoughts.

> *For as the rain cometh down, and the snow from heaven, and returneth not thither, but watereth the earth, and maketh it bring forth and bud, that it may give seed to the sower, and bread to the eater: so shall my word be that goeth forth out of my mouth: it shall not return unto me void, but it shall accomplish that which I please, and it shall prosper in the thing whereto I sent it. For ye shall go out with joy, and be led forth with peace: the mountains and the hills shall break forth before you into singing, and all the trees of the field shall clap their hands.*
> —Isa. 55:10–12 KJV

God's Word, written and spoken, is a binding, legal contract with the things He has created. The mindset of the 21st century virgin can easily get stuck due to a lack of revelation. This type of thought process can also easily place people at risk, feeling overtaken with false information. As a result, it can lead to disillusion from the truth. The 21st century virgin thought process often seeks after the presence of Jesus in religious activities rather than seeking Him daily by faith. "But without faith it is impossible to please him: for he that cometh to God must believe that he is, and that he is a rewarder of them that diligently seek him" (Heb. 11:6 KJV). A transformed mindset for the 21st century virgin will awaken deep desires to have a personal, intimate relationship with Jesus and as His bride.

In the process of taking on a bride of Christ mindset, worship is preceded by faith and hope inasmuch as it awakens the promises of our potential. Faith, hope, worship, and love illuminate steps to purpose. The seeds of greatness lie dormant before reaching their true purpose.

A CHANGED MINDSET VIEW OF THE KINGDOM OF GOD

With no sign of life or hope from the naked eye, the seed continues to appear dormant after it's been buried for days. Nevertheless, it's not until it's buried, watered, and broken that its true purpose can be revealed. As followers of Christ, there are times when our purpose may feel like it's asleep or crushed, and hope feels like it is deferred while waiting for its appointed time. "Hope deferred makes the heart sick, but *when the desire comes, it is* a tree of life" (Prov. 13:12). We must trust God's revelation and not attempt to understand it from the mindset of a 21st century virgin. God is the Potter who reshapes the clay and transforms the old into something new and pleasing in its purpose. God does not change the content in the clay to make it similar to the substance found in soil. The substance that makes up the clay has everything needed to fulfill its purpose and is empowered by God. He takes the old shape and transforms it by changing it into something better. Proverbs 3:5-6 says, "Trust in the LORD with all your heart, and lean not on your own understanding; in all your ways acknowledge Him, and He shall direct your paths."

> *The word that came to Jeremiah from the LORD: "Arise and go down to the potter's house, and there I will cause you to hear my words." Then I went down to the potter's house, and there he was, making something at the wheel. And the vessel that he made of clay was marred in the hand of potter; so he made it again into another vessel, as it seemed good to the potter to make.*
>
> —Jer. 18:1-4

The transformation of the mindset of the 21st century virgin to the bride of Christ Jesus is a process where God takes guardianship of what He has for them in His plan. Jeremiah 1:5 (NIV) says, "Before I formed you in the womb I knew you, before you were born I set you apart; I appointed you as a prophet to the nations." When God sees His people, although they are a work in progress, He sees them as finished and complete. Before our parents conceived us, God created us and knew us,

A CHANGED MINDSET

and He knew the purpose we were called to. God looks at the mindset of the 21st century virgins before transformation and change as pre-brides of Christ Jesus.

When creating a work of art, the artist sees the finished piece before it becomes a reality to others. God, the ultimate Artist, knows the end result of His Word and is therefore merciful and slow to anger. Sometimes eating an apple to get to the core can be a messy process. Getting to know what God's purpose is can also be a messy process. The artist may create a mess, but from it emerges a perfect work of art. It is often in this mess that the seeds of greatness are sown. Hebrews 11:1 tells us how faith takes control of the substance of things we hope for and at the same time it is the evidence of things not seen. Getting to the real you and understanding your true identity is a process that begins with seeking the kingdom of God. This mindset transformation is a journey or process that starts with a seed. The seeds planted in followers keep them in perfect peace and away from danger as they approach the core of who God is. The process of seeking God is similar to getting to the core of the apple. The process unfolds as layers are peeled away and the flesh of the apple is removed until the seeds are revealed and exposed. The transformation process brings you closer to the mindset of Christ. It is in the peeling away your old mindset, like the skin of an apple, where a changed mindset takes shape. The seeds of the apple are the desires God planted within us, and the flesh of the apple that surrounds the seeds is Jesus Christ. To get to the seeds, we have to first eat the flesh of the apple. As consumers, God gives us the seeds to be fruitful and to be a blessing to others, but they were never meant for our own consumption. It is hope where the purpose of the seeds is so much bigger than the seeds themselves.

We gain hope through God's revelation of Jesus Christ, the author and finisher of our faith. This hope allows our seeds to reach their full potential as apples. Upon reaching their full potential, the apples bring forth more seeds and hence more fruit for consumers. As more apples are produced, the hope is that others will know that the glory of God comes by tasting and seeing how good He is through Jesus Christ.

A CHANGED MINDSET VIEW OF THE KINGDOM OF GOD

I am the vine, you are the branches. He who abides in Me, and I in him, bears much fruit; for without Me you can do nothing. If anyone does not abide in Me, he is cast out as a branch and is withered; and they gather them and throw them into the fire, and they are burned. If you abide in Me, and My words abide in you, you will ask what you desire, and it shall be done for you. By this My Father is glorified, that you bear much fruit; so you will be My disciples.

—John 15:5–9

God often uses life's unexpected tragedies so people will know Him better by faith and in the hope that the relationship between Him and others will be intimate and personal. Unfortunately, the natural human mindset of the 21st century virgin often questions God, asks why these tragedies occur, and concludes that God is not in tune with what is really going on in our lives. I wanted to give my son Tyrone a vivid example of what it is like to trust Jesus the Living Word and as the substance of what faith is. I told him to imagine me, him, and other people watching a movie packed with suspense, drama, mystery, and action. I reminded Tyrone and the others that came along with us to see the movie that I had seen it several times before. Since I thought it was a great movie, I wanted them to see it and share the same experience I had.

As we all watch the movie, I saw a lot of knee-jerk reactions, especially when the main character fell into dangerous, close-to-death situations. It was quite obvious that Tyrone was annoyed with me because I did not react the same way he did. I also did not react the way he expected to many scenes where the main character was struggling just to stay alive. I reassured Tyrone and the others that I already knew how the movie ended. I also reminded Tyrone that I would not have had him watch a movie that would not meet his level of expectation for greatness. I said, "Tyrone, trust the process." Right in the middle of the movie and at the time the main character in the movie lost everything he worked so hard for, I purposefully feel asleep. I did that because I knew how the movie was going to end. Tyrone woke me up and said, "I can't believe you fell asleep at the point of the movie where the main character is at the worst point of his life." I reminded him again, "I know how the story ends. Keep watching. The best is yet to come."

> *Now when He [Jesus] got into a boat, His disciples followed Him. And suddenly a great tempest arose on the sea, so that the boat was covered with waves. But He was asleep. Then His disciples came to* Him *and awoke Him, saying, "Lord, save us! We are perishing!" But He said to them, "Why are you fearful, O you of little faith?" Then He arose and rebuked the winds and the sea, and there was a great calm. So the men marveled, saying, "Who can this be, that even the winds and the seas obey Him?"*
> —Matt. 8:23–27

The lesson here is that we need to understand where we are in relation to Jesus during life's unexpected storms. His followers questioned Jesus's love and ability to care for them during a storm, which caused them to lose all sense of control. Often, the 21st century virgin mindset will question God's motives and ways. As followers of Christ, we must learn to trust that He has ordered every step we take to our purpose. But most important is that He knows how the story ends.

> *For your fellowship in the gospel from the first day until now, being confident of this very thing, that He who has begun a good work in you will complete* it *until the day of Jesus Christ; just as it is right for me to think this of you all, because I have you in my heart, inasmuch as both in my chains and in the defense and confirmation of the gospel, you all are partakers with me of grace.*
> —Phil. 1:5–7

Doubt should not make you feel you're not on your way to your purpose just because the struggle is real. It is in knowing who God is that His followers are able find rest in troubled times. Many of the followers

A CHANGED MINDSET VIEW OF THE KINGDOM OF GOD

who walked with Jesus and knew He was the Son of God still couldn't see or understand at the time that the kingdom of heaven was right in front of them. Jesus tells us that He and the Father are one and that He takes all the cares of the world, even death, upon Himself. He wakes up the mindset of the 21st century virgin from a deep sleep to knowing that the best is yet to come.

With Jesus, it is a win-win situation. God so loved the world that He gave His only Son that we might build an optimal relationship with Him through Jesus. Yet still, we are often not ready to let go and allow God in. Food, clothing, and shelter are all important, but all these things will perish, and there will come a day when we realize that all that really matters is the soul and where it will take its permanent residence. "For what shall it profit a man, if he shall gain the whole world, and lose his own soul?" (Mark 8:36 KJV). We may know this intellectually, but we often fail to transition to learning to live a spiritually abundant life.

Matthew 6:33 tells us, "But seek ye first the kingdom of God, and his righteousness; and all these things shall be added unto you." It is through seeking the kingdom of God that followers have access to who God is and what their purpose is. All these things give life more abundantly. John 10:9–10 (KJV) tells us, "I am the door: by me if any man enters in, he shall be saved, and shall go in and out, and find pasture. The thief cometh not, but for to steal, and to kill, and to destroy: I am come that they might have life, and that they might have it more abundantly." How often the kingdom of God is so near, yet we fail to see it. It is at our fingertips, but it is up to the condition of our mindset or thought process whether we find it. It may appear to be a secret or a mystery, but this treasure is readily revealed to those who have a pure heart and a mind stayed on Jesus. The journey in finding the kingdom of God is impossible for us alone. Jesus and the Holy Spirit as the comforter will reveal the way during the journey to make the impossible possible.

The mindset of the bride of Christ is empowered to love the unloved and experience true joy in difficult times. The bride brings perfect peace instead of discord in time of trouble. The bride runs with endurance in the race whether or not emotions are telling the body to quit. The bride manifests the fruit of the Spirit in all situations. As emotional, intelligent followers, we have conversations with God rather than speaking at Him or to Him. To have a conversation with Him is to be in alignment with His thought process by faith.

As a child, I was often reminded by my parents to stay out of grown folks' conversations because they knew I had not yet developed the thought process or the emotional intelligence required to participate. As I matured, I initiated and facilitated conversations with grown folks. I also have the emotional intelligence as a result of a changed mindset in Christ. I now come boldly to His throne of grace to have a conversation with God as His daughter. "Let us therefore come boldly unto the throne of grace, that we may obtain mercy, and find grace to help in time of need" (Heb. 4:16 KJV). First Corinthians 13:11 says, "When I was a child, I spoke as a child, I understood as a child, I thought as a child; but when I became a man, I put away childish things." Jesus loves and desires for people to have their rightful place beside Him as His bride. A changed mindset from a 21st century virgin way of thinking to a bride of Christ Jesus thought process prepares individuals until His return. Virgins of the 21st century who are still living the struggle need to believe that the best is yet to come. God is omniscient. He already knows how the story ends for those who have a changed mindset.

FINAL NOTES

A Mindset That Fosters Intimacy

I am the bride God has created for Christ. I am created in the likeness and image of God, who is also known as I AM. Our union has always been a spiritual connection and not just a physical one. When Christ walked on earth as a man thousands of years ago, He waited patiently for the arrival of the Samaritan woman at the well. He gave her something that no man could ever give her. He gave her Himself as a source of living water and spoke life into her dry bones. Her readiness to change led to her true purpose. The intimacy that draws me to Jesus Christ is His ability to see me as His bride, pregnant with purpose before transformation yet with a mindset of a 21st century virgin. I now live and move and have my being in His Spirit. Since I have the mindset of the bride of Christ, Jesus aligns me with my purpose.

The relationship I have with God stems from a commitment not based on sacrifice but on obedience from Jesus. It was His commitment to me that is forever real, tangible, tried, and tested by the shedding of Jesus's blood. It is because of our relationship that I journeyed into the kingdom where I discovered my identity as His bride in the presence of God. His commitment gives me freedom and the empowerment I need to love God with all my heart, soul, and mind. His undying love is the cornerstone of my faith. He made me over again as a new creature, and my old mindset was reshaped and molded into a mindset of the bride Christ Jesus.

For God's glory, I entered into this personal and intimate relationship with Him. The world sees me as damaged goods; nevertheless, it is God who has chosen me in spite of my past and what others have said. His commitment to me is supported by His Word. God's eternal gift to me is Jesus, who tore down the veil that kept me separated from knowing who

A CHANGED MINDSET

I am in His eyes. By His grace and mercy, our heavenly Father created a hand-woven wedding garment to cover my faults, and He saw me as a suitable lover and bride for Christ Jesus. My former mindset needed to be left at the gate so I could submit myself to Him and surrender for the sake of righteousness as a bride of Christ Jesus. I am now free to enter into the kingdom of God. The small and narrow gate to the kingdom created a close, tight, intimate relationship with Christ. And God, who is rich in grace and mercy, sees me as part of this committed relationship of obedience for all time.

I have come to know that everything I need I already have as the bride of Christ. The mindset of the bride of Christ Jesus doesn't allow me to think I am perfect but lets me serve a God whose love for me is perfect. The Holy Spirit is the source of my strength and the force that binds me to God who empowers His bride with love, grace, and faithfulness. Having a changed mindset doesn't always tell me how the story will unfold, but it is like sitting next to Someone who already knows how the story ends.

SPECIAL THANKS

Special thanks to Rev. Howard Lee Phillips; Rev. Jeanette Phillips; Rev. Adolphys Lacey, Senior Pastor of Bethany Baptist Church; Roderick Williams; Kenneth Phillips Sr.; Dr. Kiniya Church; Amber Harper; Tyrone; Melissa; Anthony; Elizabeth; Catherine; Najee; Stephanie; Kevin; Kenneth Jr.; Alexandria; Jennifer; Christine; Caleb; Joshua; and Althea.

> "No matter what accomplishments you make, somebody helped you."
> —Althea Gibson

www.ingramcontent.com/pod-product-compliance
Lightning Source LLC
Chambersburg PA
CBHW062227080426
42734CB00010B/2055